Hiking and Walking Guide to EUROPE

Arthur Howcroft & Richard Sale

PASSPORT BOOKS

Trade Imprint of National Textbook Company
Lincolnwood, Illinois U.S.A.

This edition first published in 1984 by Passport Books, Trade Imprint of National Textbook Company, 4255 West Touhy Avenue, Lincolnwood, Illinois 60646 - 1975 U.S.A.

Copyright © 1983 by Arthur Howcroft and Richard Sale.

All rights reserved. No part of this book may be reproduced, stored in a retrieval system, or transmitted in any form, or by any means, electronic, mechanical, photocopying or otherwise, without the prior permission of National Textbook Company.

Manufactured in the United States of America.

4 5 6 7 8 9 0 ML 9 8 7 6 5 4 3 2 1

To our walking friends everywhere

CONTENTS

INTRODUCTION	1
AUSTRIA	11
BELGIUM	18
BRITISH ISLES	23
DENMARK	38
FINLAND	42
FRANCE (and Monaco)	49
GREECE	56
HOLLAND	60
ICELAND	64
ITALY	69
LIECHTENSTEIN	78
LUXEMBOURG	82
NORWAY	86
PORTUGAL	93
SPAIN (and Andorra)	98
SWEDEN	103
SWITZERLAND	109
WEST GERMANY	117
YUGOSLAVIA	124
EASTERN EUROPE	129

EUROPEAN LONG DISTANCE FOOTPATHS AND PROPOSED EXTENSIONS
SENTIERS DE GRANDE RANDONÉE   FERN WANDER WEGE

Reproduced in adapted form by permission of Deutscher Wanderverlag Dr. Mair & Schnabel & Co.

INTRODUCTION

EUROPE – sub-continent, a small part of the land-mass known as Eurasia, a grouping of nations for economic and political reasons, a cockpit in which world wars rage, home of distant ancestors. . . . Europe has meant many things to many people over the centuries, but for the walker it means – variety! And if variety is the spice of life, then Europe offers more than enough flavours to satisfy the palate of even the most discerning walker for a lifetime. From Lapland to the Mediterranean, from the west of Ireland to the Urals, there are all kinds of mountain and field paths to follow, from trails for the handicapped to the North Face of the Eiger. The very idea of rambling, hiking, *wandern* or *randonner* could be claimed as European. There is no one general term which covers exactly what these words mean except perhaps 'hill-walking', a term not in fashion at present but one which best expresses what this book is mainly about. We have set out to distil the essence of a vast amount of information and our own experience into what we hope will prove a useful starter for beginners and experienced walkers alike. The choice is yours. We can only act as signposts pointing you, we hope, in the direction of enriching experiences and memorable adventures.

The European Ramblers' Association and European Long-Distance Footpaths

The European Ramblers' Association (ERA) was founded in

1969. It was, in the main, of German inspiration and acts as an umbrella organisation for, to date, 36 ramblers' and mountaineering associations in 18 European countries representing a total of 1.6 million members. The ERA's main aims are:

To encourage and develop rambling and mountaineering activities;

To protect the natural environment;

To make rambling across national frontiers easier by the reduction of regulations;

To contribute, above all, through its activities to greater understanding between nations.

To further these aims, the ERA has set up a network of European Long-Distance Footpaths (LDFPs), known as E-paths. At present, there are six:

E-1 – North Sea–Lake Constance–Gotthard–Mediterranean (Flensburg–Constance–Genoa) = 2 450 km (1 530 miles)

E-2 – Holland/Belgium–Mediterranean (Berg op Zoom/Ostend–Geneva–Nice) = 2 376 km (1 485 miles)

E-3 – Atlantic–Ardennes–Bohemian Forest (Royan–Luxembourg–Marktredwitz) = 2 295 km (1 430 miles)

E-4 – Pyrenees–Jura–Neusiedlersee (Bourg-Madame–Constance–Rust) = 2 604 km (1 628 miles)

E-5 – Lake Constance–Adriatic (Constance–Bolzano–Venice) = 600 km (375 miles)

E-6 – Baltic Sea–Bohemian Forest–Wachau–Adriatic (Copenhagen–Lübeck–Mariazell–Rijeka) = 2 816 km (1 760 miles)

These international paths link existing national paths. Extensions to them, and a seventh path, are being planned by the ERA's Wegkommission (Footpaths Commission). Guides for each of the existing E-paths are available (in

German only at present) from Deutscher Wanderverlag and Fink Verlag at specialist map shops (see Useful Addresses for each country.)

The encouragement and development of actual walking activities on these and other footpaths is largely the concern of the ERA's Wanderkommission (Walking Commission). This collects and disseminates information about the opportunities offered by the member-organisations to walk and holiday with them in their respective countries. A brochure *Ferienwanderungen in Deutschland und Europa* (Walking Holidays in Germany and Europe) is published every year and is available from ERA headquarters.

Other projects in the pipeline are:

Guidelines for requesting information from abroad – this will be a standardised letter in several languages which will enable you to obtain walking information from the country you wish to visit.

An International Walkers' Vocabulary of words and phrases useful for interpreting guides and getting around abroad.

A Personal Advisory Service Scheme for Visitors from Abroad – a network of individuals who would be willing to help and/or walk with you when you are in their country or area. (If *you* would like to help in this, please let us know.)

Finally, the ERA is moving into the field of environmental protection. Concern for the natural environment should be a priority for everyone and we hope that the more you walk in it the more you too will become concerned.

Grading of walks

Unfortunately there is as yet no internationally accepted

grading of walks. The Austrians have developed a 'difficulty grading' (*Schwierigskeitgrad*) for their paths and this is used in many German guidebooks too. Briefly, it is as follows:

A & B – *Easy*. Paths cross level or gently undulating terrain. Altitude differences less than 250 m (800 ft). Suitable for families with young children, and can be walked in any weather.

C – *Moderate*. Paths cross hilly terrain and mountains up to 1 800 m (6 000 ft). Altitude differences less than 600 m (2 000 ft). Route-finding fairly straightforward. Paths not difficult except in extremely bad weather.

D – *Difficult*. Paths may ascend or descend for considerable distances and cross steep, marshy or rocky terrain. Sometimes above treeline, sometimes not altogether clear. Not difficult to follow in *good weather* for experienced walkers who know how to use map and compass. Check locally if at all doubtful.

E – *Very Difficult*. Routes are strenuous and cross rough terrain with steep ascents and descents. Map and compass skills very necessary. No specific climbing skills and equipment necessary in good weather but could be useful in bad weather. A 'head for heights' is occasionally needed on some sections, even when these have safeguards such as fixed cables and ladders. *Not* recommended for beginners and young children.

F – *Extremely Difficult*. Routes cross glaciers and steep exposed sections without safeguards. Mountaineering skills (map and compass, glacier work, rock-climbing to grade II – difficult) and equipment (ice-axe, crampons, rope) are often necessary. To be avoided unless very experienced, or with guides.

If you are uncertain about your, or your companion's, capabilities with regard to difficulty we suggest you attempt a grade lower than you think you are capable of. The same is true of distance walking – take it in smaller steps than you think you can do. A good indicator is not the *distance* but the *time* you can walk comfortably. The (mainly continental) habit of thinking that point A is so many hours away is one we cannot urge too strongly on you if you wish to walk abroad. You will only know, of course, when you have tried – and probably pushed yourself up to or beyond your limit.

There are, of course, an almost infinite number of ways of hill-walking, from going out alone (for the *very* experienced only and they almost never do it!) to participating in mass walks for charity (a special case not regarded altogether favourably by regular walkers). Many people find the greatest satisfaction in a good day out on the hills with one or a few like-minded friends. Others find the 'club outing', organised and with 'official' leaders, is best for them. Most major national walking organisations at home and abroad (see Useful Addresses) have local groups and if you are a beginner – and even if you are not – you will probably find one nearby which will be only too willing to welcome you and enlarge your experience of the hills.

For longer periods, a walking holiday can take several forms. The walking tour, moving on from day to day and backpacking all you need for camping, hostelling or overnighting in huts, hotels etc., is very popular. Less demanding from the weight-carrying point of view is the centre holiday where you stay at one or more centres and go out on day excursions. You can of course plan your own holiday in either case or else take a package holiday offered by the many organisations now active both here and elsewhere. We have tried to indicate the major reliable organisations that will help you, whichever way you choose to 'go out on the hill'.

Equipment (mainly for beginners)

In the welter of equipment now available perhaps the best advice is *do not overbuy*. Old clothes are sufficient provided they keep you *warm* and keep out the elements. Never forget that *wind* is the main enemy so that wind-proofing rather than waterproofing is first priority. Some items of equipment should be considered as essential:

Boots (nearly always preferable to shoes). These are the major requirement. Make sure they fit well when you have your normal complement of socks on, and buy the best you can afford.

Anoraks. As all-purpose garments they are hard to beat and a good investment.

Warm Clothing. Most modern garments work on the 'air-trap' principle, creating protective layers of warm air inside to keep you warm. This means that several layers of thin clothing are better than one thick layer of equal weight. Finally, remember that wool is still hard to beat.

Waterproofs. Shell clothing (normally nylon), if completely waterproof, creates condensation and can make you wetter than rain. The new 'breathing' materials on the market are very good but expensive, and remember that they let air out so you feel colder in bad weather.

Go to a specialist shop and ask for their help if you are not sure. If they are good – most of them are – they will be more concerned with helping you enjoy the hills than with ruining your bank-balance.

Hill-craft and route-finding

On the European mainland, most major, and minor, paths are waymarked. Even so, the ability to use a map and compass is a vital requirement. It might save your life; it will certainly add to the pleasure of travelling in the hills. There are many books written on the subject of route-finding, but in the long run the only real teacher is experience. Read the books by all means but practise whenever you can, preferably in good weather, until you are sure you can cope. One final point — unless you know there are magnetic rocks about, trust your compass! You may have a splendid sense of direction, but your compass has a better one.

Hazards

If you are careful about your equipment, acquiring experience patiently and choosing your areas and seasons with discernment (we have given a few indicators in the text), you face no very great danger in Europe. Wild animals are not normally dangerous in any of the countries mentioned. Indeed the worst hazard is likely to be an unfriendly bull in Britain! Deer in the rutting season are best avoided, but otherwise you will encounter wild animals only rarely or if you are deliberately looking for them.

Rabies is now endemic practically everywhere on mainland Europe but, thankfully, not yet in Great Britain. Some sensible precautions can be taken:

do not tangle with unknown dogs or cats even if they appear to be friendly;

avoid any wild animals (foxes especially) if they appear to be behaving abnormally;

be careful about semi-tame animals that come to be fed — even a nut-gathering squirrel can be rabid and a scratch and certainly a nip can be dangerous.

If you are at all suspicious of a bite or scratch from any animal you *must* seek medical advice and treatment *at once*. A description of the animal, its behaviour and its location or, not so easy, the animal itself should be taken along. Remember, the incubation period for rabies can be as long as six months, so a bite or scratch *must not* be ignored because it 'gets better'. Remember finally that wild berries are often eaten and *can be contaminated* by rabid animals, so please try to resist the temptation in rabies-prone areas to gorge yourself on those wild strawberries or bilberries glistening in the sunlight – they could be the last meal you really enjoy.

Snakes Dangers from poisonous snakes in Europe are usually exaggerated. Seven species of poisonous snake – all vipers – exist in Europe but are not known in Ireland, Corsica and Crete. The common viper or adder occurs in the cooler areas of Europe, being the only poisonous snake in Scandinavia (except Iceland and the far north), Britain (except Ireland), the Benelux countries and Germany. The asp viper occurs in southern France, eastern Spain and Italy, the nose-horned viper in states on the eastern Adriatic coastline and Greece, the Ottoman viper on the Asia Minor boundary, while the blunt-nosed viper is limited to a small number of Greek islands. While no viper bite is trivial it is these five named snakes that have bites which, if untreated, can be fatal to man, the last four being considered the most dangerous.

If someone is bitten, forget what you have seen Gary Cooper do in films! *Do not* cut and suck as this causes more distress to an already distressed victim. Keep the victim calm and as still as is practical and get him medical treatment as fast as possible. The only effective treatment is anti-snake-bite serum. Kits are available, if you know how to use them, and are recommended in certain areas. Finally, remember that encounters with snakes are very rare, and bites even rarer. If you are wearing boots and thick socks you should be fairly safe even if you nearly tread on one. The snake will certainly be more frightened than you at such a time, and will only strike in self-defence.

Insects are more of a nuisance than a hazard. Stinging insects are pain-causing but very rarely fatal. Mosquitoes are probably the biggest nuisance, particularly in hot, damp, marshy areas. If you react badly to insects, you can try insect-repellents. Our, not very encouraging, experience in this respect indicates that there are two kinds – those that do not work and those that attract even more insects! Sometimes if you ignore them they bother you less, sometimes it is better to choose, if possible, another time of year to visit the area in question. We have tried to indicate recommended walking seasons in the text.

Drinking water is less of a problem than it used to be because of recent policies for pure water by European international organisations. Even so, there are occasional problems. Check locally, and if in any doubt at all, consider boiling all water to be used for consumption or use water-purifying tablets. Finally, remember that it is most unwise to drink from a glacial stream or river, as the cold, silt-filled water can easily induce stomach cramp and worse.

Language difficulties

These do occur, but in most of western Europe and Scandinavia you will almost certainly find someone sooner or later who understands and speaks English. Younger people in particular are likely to be most helpful practically everywhere. It is useful, however, and often a great help, to be able at least to greet people in their own language and to be able to ask for food and directions and to count. After English you will find the most widely understood languages are French, German, Spanish and Italian in that order.

Finally, remember that there is no need to shout – unless an emergency makes you feel that you must.

Useful addresses and telephone numbers

We have tried to ensure that these are as correct and up-to-date as possible. For all telephone numbers, we have given the area code in brackets, but check the code before use, especially if phoning from another country.

Despite these cautionary notes we want finally to say that walking abroad in Europe is not at all difficult unless you care to make it so. If this book helps to start you on the pathway to happy times and experiences at all similar to those that we have had, then our efforts have been worth while.

So get out and about and walking abroad!

Schone Wandertage!
Bonnes Randonnées!
Buon Randunno!
Bergheil!

AUSTRIA

(OESTERREICH)

LAND of mountains and music where the women wear elaborate dirndl skirts and the men in leather shorts and feathered hats drink beer, yodel and play zithers, is probably the standard tourist image of Austria. It is not entirely wrong. Over 70 per cent of the country is mountainous and traditional ways of life are still maintained, not without a certain amount of pride, in most parts of Austria, even in the larger towns and cities. Austrian cooking with its great variety of *Schnitzel*, *Apfelstrudel* and *Kuchen* is still to be had everywhere with good beer or excellent white wine, most likely from the region around Vienna, as splendid accompaniment. And it would be a rare visitor who did not have the opportunity at least once in his or her stay to enjoy an evening of music, song and dance.

For the Austrians, tourism is a serious business done with a great sense of enjoyment. They know what brings tourists to their country and are doing their best to hold on to and promote the good things that do bring them.

For walkers this means that almost everywhere they can be sure of a warm welcome and ample opportunities to walk at all grades of difficulty (see the Introduction for the Austrian grading of walks). Whilst the most popular area is undoubtedly the Tyrol, there are mountains galore in the provinces of Vorarberg, Salzburg, Carinthia and Styria. Even Vienna in the lower part of the country has its Vienna Woods. And because, in general, the Austrian Alps are lower than their Swiss and French counterparts – highest peak Gross Glockner at 3 798 m (12 457 ft) – walkers have been able to take their first steps above the snowline in Austria towards more serious mountaineering elsewhere, or, not surprisingly, in Austria again and again.

Arguably, then, Austria offers walkers some of the richest experiences and enjoyment to be had on the mainland of Europe. It is not a country to neglect or ignore.

Walking in Austria

For most Austrians, the mountains and mountain-walking are quite simply a part of life. The provision made for walking reflects this to a remarkable degree.

A very fully developed footpath network exists with 10 major LDFPs (that is, Long-Distance Footpaths or *Weitwanderwege*) crossing the country in all directions. Some sections of these paths are also used as part of the three European LDFPs (E-4, E-5 and E-6) that cross through Austria. The *Weitwanderwege* are numbered from 01 to 10 and are often named as well. The 01, the Nordalpenweg, for instance, starts at Bregenz on Lake Constance and traverses the whole country to Vienna, a distance of 1 400 km (875 miles). It is also the alpine variation of the E-4 which path also has a lowland variation further north, from Salzburg to Vienna.

From each of the major paths, 01, 02 etc., regional paths, numbered 101, 102 etc., interconnect and make other long-distance or circular routes possible. The Pielachtaler Rundweitwanderung route number 652, for instance, is a five-day circuit to the south-west of St Polten in Lower Austria.

Paths are mostly very well waymarked with paint marks on rocks, trees etc., and numbers and signposts where other paths intersect. The major organisation responsible for the upkeep and continued development of this network, as for much else in the Austrian mountains, is the Austrian Alpine Club (see Useful Addresses at chapter end).

Maps and guides

A guidebook to each of the 10 major official paths is published by the Austrian Alpine Club. There are also numerous other guides to both these and other routes available from other publishers, but at present they are all in German. A good general guide for starters is *Mountain Rambles in Austria*, available in English from the Austrian National Tourist Office (see Useful Addresses). Local tourist offices in Austria, even in quite small villages, often have information about suggested walks in their area and this often appears on the backs of special tourist maps which the tourist offices design and publish themselves. Sometimes these will have versions and/or keys in English. Most guides include information about the countryside the path traverses, local history, customs, places of interest, accommodation etc., but of course knowledge of German is really necessary to get the best out of such guides.

Walking maps are readily available; the most popular are:

Touristenwanderkarten by Freytag-Berndt, scale 1:100 000. Many of these have information about huts, approaches to them and interconnecting routes with walking times on the back or on the cover. Freytag-Berndt also publish larger-scale maps, 1:50 000, for the most popular mountain areas.

Alpenvereinskarten, at 1:25 000, are published by the Austrian Alpine Club and are the most detailed maps available for the most important mountain ranges. The AAC also publishes *Alpenvereinshütten in den Ostalpen* at 1:500 000 which shows all the club huts in Austria. It can be useful for preliminary planning and can be bought from the club and many bookshops.

Oesterreichische Karten, at 1:50 000, are the official 'Ordnance Survey' type maps. They come in rigidly divided quadrants so that three may be needed for a 10 km walk. Not the most useful for walkers, but if you do buy them make sure they are *mit Wegmarkierung*, i.e. with waymarking.

Kompass Wanderkarten, at 1:50 000, cover the mountain areas but not all the lower sections of Austria. There are enlarged 1:25 000 versions for the most popular areas.

Overnighting

Hotels of all grades exist in towns and villages and are generally of a high standard. The *Gasthof* or *Gasthaus* title usually implies something not so grand and probably appeals most to walkers. As in Germany, *Privatzimmer* or *Zimmer zu vermieten* – rooms in private houses – signs are worth investigating by small groups or individuals and both they and larger groups will nearly always get considerable help in finding accommodation from the local tourist office. Out on the mountains, sometimes at considerable altitudes, the Alpine Club huts are to be found. These huts, mostly wardened and set at 3–8 hours walking time from each other, form the best-developed chain of overnight lodgings in the whole of the Alps. 'Huts' is something of a misnomer since many are like hotels. If you arrive early enough, and a club member who has priority booking does not, you may manage a bedroom. If not, then dormitory accommodation, *Matrazenlager*, will usually be available, as will quite elaborate meals at a surprisingly modest cost. At the most luxurious huts you will even find electric light and hot showers. It is hardly surprising that the 'hut tour' is one of the most popular ways of travelling through the Austrian mountains, but don't be surprised if at busy times two hundred other walkers have had the same idea! If you are in a party of six or more, booking in advance is strongly recommended.

Camping is officially allowed on approved sites only and is forbidden in conservation areas. Local tourist offices hold lists of the approved sites, and the forbidden areas. Camping near mountain-huts is not welcomed and in many areas just not allowed even if the hut is bulging.

Recommended walking areas

Vorarlberg, Tyrol, Salzburg and Carinthia (Kärnten) have already been mentioned and are easily the most popular. Certain valleys in the Tyrol, the Stubaital, Ötztal, and Zillertal, become uncomfortably overcrowded in the high season, as do the mountain ranges that surround them. This may be the time to explore smaller and lower ranges and valleys in Styria (Steiermark) and Lower Austria (Niederösterreich) where tourism has not yet got such a hold. Upper Austria (Oberösterreich) offers the Totes Gebirge or the Böhmerwald and Salzburg Province, the Salzkammergut, fine lakeland country, but rain is a hazard frequently met with in these areas.

Climate

This is of course essentially Alpine and Central European and therefore unpredictable. In summer it can be very hot for long periods at a time but it can rain, not usually for as long, and thunderstorms, sometimes very violent, occur. In winter the temperature can remain below freezing point for long periods, good for skiing. Late June and early July and September–October are recommended if you can possibly go then.

Hazards

None beyond those mentioned in the Introduction except perhaps stonefall and avalanches in certain parts of the higher mountains. Ask the locals or read the guides carefully if in doubt. Alcohol is a considerable hazard if you care to make it one, or get in well with an Austrian party!

Language

English is widely spoken in the most popular tourist areas. In the more remote areas, even if you think you know German, you may have problems. This is because the Austrians, especially older ones, speak dialects with strong and unfamiliar intonations so that even some Germans cannot easily understand them! You will usually get by with patience and will nearly always be received with warm goodwill whatever the language difficulty.

Useful addresses

>Austrian National Tourist Office
>545 Fifth Ave.
>New York, NY 10017   Tel: (212) 679-0651

also Fremdenverkehrsamt *(local tourist office) of the province, town or village you wish to visit*

>Österreichischer Alpenverein (ÖAV)
>Wilhelm Greil Strasse 15
>A-6010 Innsbruck. Tel: (05222) 23171

for maps, hut information and information on mountaineering courses

Deutscher Alpenverein
Praterinsel 5
München 22
West Germany. Tel: (089) 29 30 86
runs some club huts

Österreichischer Touristenklub (ÖTK)
Bäckerstrasse 16
A 1010 Wien. Tel: (0222) 52 38 44
has some huts and runs climbing courses

Touristenverein 'Die Naturfreunde' (TVN)
Viktoriagasse 6
A 1150 Wien. Tel: (0222) 83 86 08
has some huts

Österreichische Fremdenverkehrswerbung
Margaretenstrasse 1
A 1040 Wien 4. Tel: (0222) 57 57 14/15
for camping and general information in Austria

BELGIUM

(BELGIQUE, BELGIE)

SEASIDE resorts with almost familiar names like Ostend and De Panne; old, solidly built towns like Bruges (or Brugge) and Ghent (or Gand) and, above all, for the British, Waterloo, are perhaps the first images conjured up by the mention of Belgium. These are likely to be closely followed by Brussels (and the EEC) and perhaps unclear memories of train journeys from Ostend or Zeebrugge across a darkening, rather flat and dull agricultural landscape, none of which has much to inspire the walker who wants to explore Belgium.

The truth is somewhat different. The coast has some interesting sand-dune country with, further inland and to the north, heath, bog and pine forest, whilst the central plateau (up to 200 m, 650 ft) has some beautiful river valleys and, of greatest interest to the walker, the south-east offers the very ancient Ardennes plateau.

Walking in Belgium

Whilst there have always been keen enthusiasts to go *wandeln* or *randonner* in Belgium, the walking organisations have really 'taken off' since the seventies. The testimony to their activity is a growing network of footpaths very similar to the French system on which it is based. As might be expected, a Flemish-speaking organisation, Grote Routepaden (GR), promotes footpaths mainly in Flanders and a French-speaking sister organisation, the Comité National Belge des

Sentiers de Grande Randonnée (CNBSGR), looks after footpath development in the French-speaking part of Belgium, Walloon. Fortunately for the visiting walker, co-operation rather than conflict, all too familiar in other aspects of Belgian life, is their watchword. You are sure of a warm response if you contact either of them (see Useful Addresses).

As already indicated, the Belgians have constructed a series of *sentiers de grande randonnée* (SGR) or *lange afstandswandelwegen* across their country that link not only with the French but also with the Dutch, German and Luxembourg LDFPs. Thus it is possible to start on the Belgian coast and continue right across national borders to create walks that are truly international. Small linking sections, shorter routes and, in particular, circular routes branch off from the major system and offer ample opportunities for practically all grades of walking.

The GR 5, for instance, forms part of the European LDFP E-2 from Holland to the Mediterranean and, with a major variation, the GR 5A, crosses the whole country from the North Sea coast to the Ardennes. From it the GR 57 explores the valleys of the river Ourthe whilst the GR 577 is a 65 km (40 mile) circuit of the valleys of the Lesse and the Lomme. A special path, designated GR AE, is the Ardennes – Eifel LDFP which links Belgium with Luxembourg and Germany.

As in France, white and red bars are used to denote the correct LDFP route, a variety of signs being used elsewhere.

Maps and Guides

Topo-guides are available from local tourist offices, especially those on the major footpath routes, and the two organisations GR and CNBSGR normally hold all of them in stock. The guides are in French or Flemish depending largely on which part of the country they describe. They are very similar to French topo-guides with descriptions of the route, the surrounding countryside, accommodation etc.

Maps in scales of 1:25 000 and 1:50 000 are published by the Institut Géographique National in Brussels (see Useful Addresses) and local tourist offices often issue special maps showing, and/or describing, walks in their area. GR also publish 1:100 000 maps of each province showing the LDFPs.

Both GR and CNBSGR publish quarterly bulletins, *GR Berichten* and *GR Informations*, which are available by subscription and which contain useful up-to-date information.

In some provinces, route descriptions of particularly attractive paths are published. This is particularly true of Namur, on the GR 12 LDFP from Brussels to Paris and other long-distance routes. The Fédération du Tourisme de la Province de Namur (FTPN, see Useful Addresses) publishes not only some very interesting guides but also a regular programme of walks which you would be welcome to join if you were there at the right time. Do not be in too much of a hurry – the provincial symbol is a snail!

As yet, the information about such walks is not available in English.

Overnighting

Hotels of all grades exist in Belgium, but in the country many modest and simple hotels make ample provision for the walker. The Belgian National Tourist Office supplies a list of budget accommodation.

Recently, the Association Belge des Auberges de la Jeunesse – Vlaamse Jeugdhebergcentral (VZW, the Belgian

YHA) – has made great strides in providing more and better youth hostels. They might well be worth investigating if they lie on your route.

Camping is allowed on official sites and a list of sites, in the form of a map, is available from the Belgian National Tourist Office.

Recommended walking areas

Coastal Plain and Central Plateau – In addition to the GR 5/5A section and the GR 12 Brussels–Paris, the GR 121 (Ronse to Boulogne, France) is worthwhile.

Namur Province – The areas of the Sambre–Meuse plateaux and Ardennes foothills have many designated routes.

Liège Province – The valley of the Ourthe and the Ardennes. Particularly recommended are the area around Malmédy (Belgium's highest peak, Botrange, 694 m (2 276 ft), is not too far away) and the area to the east and south which form the North Eifel–Hautes Fagne Nature Park, a joint German–Belgian project.

Climate

Temperate in the main, but rainfall can be quite heavy and frequent on the coast with thunderstorms farther east. Winters can be quite severe in the Ardennes, but late spring and early autumn are often fine and the best times to walk.

Hazards

No serious hazards beyond those mentioned in the Introduction. Belgian drivers used to be considered a hazard on roads, but there are signs of improving standards. Food and drink are often copious in Belgium — dieters beware!

Language

Belgian French is said to make the French squirm but it is often spoken more slowly, which might help your ill-remembered school French a great deal.

Flemish (Dutch) sounds like a language you nearly know, because it often seems like a mixture of English and German. If you listen carefully you may be able to make out quite a lot. If not, you will usually find a Belgian who speaks more than passable English.

Useful addresses

>Belgium National Tourist Office
>745 Fifth Ave.
>New York, NY 10020 Tel: (212) 758-8130
>
>Comité National Belge des Sentiers de Grande Randonnée (CNBSGR)
>BP 10
>4000 Liège
>
>*or*
>12 rue des Eschasseurs
>5000 Namur
>
>Grote Routepaden (and Flemish YHA)
>Van Stralenstraat 40
>2000 Antwerpen. Tel: (31) 232 72 18
>
>Fédération du Tourisme de la Province de Namur
>3 rue Notre Dame
>5000 Namur. Tel: (81) 222998
>
>Institut Géographique National
>3 Abbaye de la Cambre
>1050 Bruxelles. Tel: (2) 6485282

THE BRITISH ISLES

(1: ENGLAND, WALES and SCOTLAND)

Many people have misleading ideas about Great Britain. Hikers and walkers are no exception. Over the years they have seen Great Britain as, on the one hand, simply a training ground for sterner stuff abroad, on the other, simply the best place in the world for walking. Misconceptions about all the British Isles are even greater. Great Britain is small in area: how can it take a whole day to travel from London to Scotland? The cities sprawl into gigantic conurbations: how can Britain look so green from the air? The 'mountains', with Ben Nevis, the highest peak, a mere 1 343 m (4 406 ft) are not really to be taken seriously: how can they possibly kill so many people every year? And of course it is always foggy — or raining...

When visitors come from abroad, especially those who come to walk, they are most often pleasantly surprised. There is much more open space than they thought, it is often easy to get out of the cities quickly into open and very beautiful countryside, the mountains are 'real mountains' in shape if not in height, and the fog lifts often enough to reveal marvellous vistas over hill and dale and – best of all – the sea.

What impresses visitors most is the great variety of landscape that exists in a relatively small compass – which makes Britain in this respect a Europe in miniature, and something else besides. Walkers, yearning perhaps for sunnier climes on occasion, would do well to remember that and take every opportunity to explore this rich variety.

It is traditional to divide Great Britain into lowlands, south and east of a line from the river Tees to the Exe, and uplands to the north and west of this line. Walkers need not bother too much about this division. With everything on offer from nature trails to long-distance footpaths, from gentle downland walking to routes requiring ice-axes and ropes in winter, they will find enough to satisfy them for a lifetime.

Walking in Great Britain

There are more than 193 000 km (120 000 miles) of public footpaths in Britain of which some 2 400 km (1 500 miles) are officially recognised LDFPs. Basically footpaths are the responsibility of local authorities, who vary in their commitment and ability to maintain them. The question is complicated by the fact that many – perhaps most – footpaths cross private land so that constant vigilance has to be maintained to ensure that they continue to exist. The LDFPs, officially recognised by the government's Countryside Commission, are now sufficiently well established, but others are not always safe and can and do disappear unless a watch is kept on the whole network.

The unofficial watchdog, constantly fighting to maintain and extend the network, is the Ramblers' Association (RA) supported by other amenity bodies. Through their local groups, these associations manage to keep access to much of the countryside open for everyone to enjoy. You can write to the Ramblers' Association for information about their activities (see Useful Addresses).

Partly as a result of their efforts, a whole series of unofficial (i.e. non-recognised) LDFPs exist almost everywhere. They are made up from existing paths, go through some of the finest countryside and sometimes link one area with another. There is likely to be one not too far away from you which may be well worth investigating and following.

In England and Wales, there are 10 National Parks, designated by the Countryside Commission, which cover nearly one-tenth of the country and contain some of the most beautiful countryside still in existence. Unlike national parks in many other countries, where the land is state-owned, these parks are mostly private property. Access to open space within them and consequent 'freedom to roam' is therefore something you must always ascertain before setting off across an apparently empty but very alluring tract of open countryside. Good relationships with farmers and landowners need to be encouraged and are not always made easy by forays of this kind, no matter how lacking in malice they may seem. Maps and signs will tell you when and where you are on a public path or have reached an access point and it would help if you used them whenever you can. The 'Country Code' issued by the Countryside Commission and fully supported by the amenity bodies is something you should know and respect everywhere and at all times.

In addition to the National Parks, there are a number of Areas of Outstanding Natural Beauty (AONBs) where beautiful countryside is partly protected and conservation is encouraged. LDFPs and other paths are to be found in all of them and elsewhere.

Signposting of footpaths is not consistent, although many local authorities are now using green metal or wooden signposts at the beginnings and ends of paths. The signs usually give the distance, more and more often in kilometres, to a particular destination. You should not expect waymarking throughout the length of the trails and will almost certainly have to use a map and a compass too on occasion when out walking them.

Finally, it has to be said that the pressure on the British countryside, which diminishes in area every year, is growing all the time. This brings its particular problems for walkers: getting away from it all is not always easy, especially at holiday times and weekends, other countryside users disturb your peace, and the paths sometimes become very badly eroded mud slides or bare, stony, stumbling, even leg-breaking trials of endurance.

Even so, walking in the British Isles is still highly enjoyable. More and more people seem to think so if the number out and about is any guide. Why not join them if you have not already done so?

Maps and guides

A byword for accuracy and used by generations of walkers, the maps published by the Ordnance Survey are still irreplaceable. There are several series. The 1:50 000 Landranger Series (purple cover) have all footpaths marked. The 1:25 000 First Series (blue cover) is not always up-to-date but a Second Series (green cover) is gradually being published and is subject to constant revision. A special series of 1:25 000 Outdoor Leisure maps of the major recreational areas is also being published and these are the ones to look for first.

Some special maps, often based on the Ordnance Survey, are also published by various private and commercial enterprises. They are most easily found in the area they cover and may prove useful on occasion.

Guides, too numerous to mention individually, are appearing in ever growing numbers. The LDFPs are covered by 'official' guides published by Her Majesty's Stationery Office (HMSO) but there are many 'non-official' – sometimes better – guides to these paths too. Most of the 'non-official' footpaths or 'ways' mentioned on page 24 also have guides published sooner or later. There are also guides to whole areas and walking from towns or villages, usually obtainable locally.

If you intend to walk in an area you have not visited before, the best plan is to go to your local equipment shop or your nearest large bookshop, and start with the OS map and/or any guide that seems to tell you what you want to know. You will almost certainly find others as your planning and your walking proceed. Try not to be overwhelmed by the sheer volume of what is available.

Overnighting

Hotels exist at all standards in Britain. Some welcome walkers with open arms, others find their muddy boots highly undesirable and turn them away. In the popular walking areas a warm welcome is usual, but not inevitable. Check before you book.

Better for walkers are the more modest farmhouses, inns and – the institutions which delight foreign visitors – bed and breakfast places. Overnight stops at such places are part of the excitement of a walking tour, but in busy periods and areas do try to book in advance.

In addition to these, some 300 youth hostels form a splendid network of overnight stops for members, nearly always within walking distance of each other in the popular areas. There is no age limit and hostelling holidays are a rather special experience highly recommended. (See Useful Addresses for details of the Youth Hostels Association.)

Centre walking holidays of a more organised nature are offered from the guest houses of the Countrywide Holidays Association (CHA), Holiday Fellowship (HF) and Ramblers' Association (RA).

There are no 'official' camp sites in Britain but a large number of private ones and a few run by the National Park bodies do exist. The local tourist office or the Camping Club of Great Britain (see Useful Addresses) are your best first sources for information.

Recommended walking areas

All the national parks and AONBs offer worthwhile walking, as does much of the coast outside these areas. In the north, the Lakes, Yorkshire Dales and Peak District are the most visited. In the south, Dartmoor and Exmoor are the most popular. In Wales, Snowdonia and the Brecon Beacons have this dubious distinction.

There are other areas that await 'discovery' by walkers: Mid-Wales, the Cotswolds, the Trough of Bowland and many others, but do not be too surprised if other walkers have discovered them before you!

Scotland needs a special mention. There are no national parks, and only two LDFPs, one of which is complete, have been designated. This has not prevented Scotland from becoming a, if not the, firm favourite for many walkers. The Border country and all areas north of the Forth and the Clyde offer some of the finest scenery and last wilderness areas to be found in Britain. Remember, however, that the hazards increase as you go further north (see page 29).

Climate

'If you can see the hills, it's going to rain, and if you can't, it's raining' is almost a maxim for British walkers. What this really means is that the climate is extremely changeable, one particular kind of weather rarely lasting for more than forty-eight hours anywhere. Sometimes, prolonged periods of rain do set in and sometimes – more rarely, it seems – fine weather can last for weeks. The variety of weather almost matches the variety of the landscape. It can be cold, especially in the uplands in winter. It is, however, rarely too hot anywhere for walking, even in the summer. The only thing to do is to accept the weather and always go out *prepared*.

Best walking seasons: spring to autumn but avoid late July and August if you can.

Hazards

Apart from a few snakes and bulls in fields, mentioned in the Introduction, the major hazards come from the terrain and the changeable weather. This combination has caught and still catches walkers out, sometimes with fatal results. It is worth remembering that Kinder Scout in the Peak District, a mere 600 m (2 000 ft) high, is nearly at the same latitude as the Canadian Great Lakes and can be a white-out wasteland in winter. Nearly every year somebody falls off ice on Snowdon – and that as late as Easter. Even the Quantocks in Somerset can produce spring snowstorms of surprising ferocity.

Scotland again needs a special mention. As in Norway, mountains often start at or near sea-level so that the scale of the land is much greater in reality than it appears on the map. Winter comes early and snow lies late (Ben Nevis is just below the permanent snow-line). In winter, conditions can become arctic in less than an hour.

Finally, the need for good map-reading in the British Isles must be emphasised. For all sorts of reasons, British paths, though often cairned, are not as fully signposted or waymarked as those in mainland Europe. Route-finding is part of the fun and adventure and is partly the reason why Britain produces so many outstanding mountaineers and explorers. Try at least to emulate them even if you do not become one.

Language

Dialects are the only real difficulty, as anyone listening to a Geordie and a Devonian together will tell you!

If you are not English-speaking, remember that the British are supposed to be poor linguists. Not entirely true, but not entirely false either. . . .

Useful addresses

British Tourist Authority
680 Fifth Ave.
New York, NY 10019   Tel: (212) 581-4700

The Countryside Commission
John Dower House
Crescent Place
Cheltenham GL50 3RA. Tel: (0242) 21381
for general information about National Parks and LDFPs etc.

Ramblers' Association
1/5 Wandsworth Road
London SW8 2LJ. Tel: (01) 582 6878
for general information on walking in Britain, local groups, a very useful Bed and Breakfast Guide and much else besides

Youth Hostels Association (YHA)
Trevelyan House
8 St Stephens Hill
St Albans
Herts AL1 2DY. Tel: (0727) 55215
with shops in London, Manchester, Birmingham and Cardiff – lots of information (not only hostelling) and equipment

Scottish Youth Hostels Association (SYHA)
7 Glebe Crescent
Stirling FK8 2JA. Tel: (0786) 2821
for hostelling and holidays in Scotland

Camping Club of Great Britain and Ireland Ltd
11 Lower Grosvenor Place
London SW1W 0EY. Tel: (01) 828 9232
for information on camping

Her Majesty's Stationery Office (HMSO)
49 High Holborn
London. Tel: (01) 928 6977

or (mailorder)
HMSO
PO Box 569
London SE1 9NH. Tel: as above
for maps, LDFP guides and Countryside Commission publications. HMSO also has shops in major cities.

THE BRITISH ISLES

(2: NORTHERN IRELAND and EIRE)

THE 'Emerald Isle', famed in fable and song, has had more than its fair share of bad publicity recently. From the walker's point of view, this is a great pity. The island abounds in walking opportunities everywhere. Ireland is essentially saucer-shaped with an undulating limestone plain mixed with peat and clay in the centre surrounded by hills, sometimes dome-shaped granite as in the east in the Wicklow and Mourne Mountains, sometimes more ridge-like sandstone as in the south and west in Kerry and Cork, sometimes jagged quartzite as in Connemara. And since nowhere in Ireland is more than 112 km (70 miles) from the sea, coastal walking is nearly always possible. Indeed, Ireland has some of the remotest and wildest unspoilt cliff scenery left in the British Isles, and of course the Giant's Causeway is a 'must' for anyone even faintly interested in geology.

Away from the 'hot-spots', life still goes on in the same timeless unhurried way. Everyone has time for a chat and a helping hand when you meet them – so much time, in fact, that the consequent delays might almost be considered a hazard to the completion of a walk! Ireland is making an immense effort in providing for visiting tourists, especially walkers: try to take advantage of it as soon as you can.

Walking in Ireland

Two Irishmen of our acquaintance are on record as 'only coming on the tour [in the Alps and very strenuous] because we had a fit of adventure!' Such 'fits of adventure' have taken many Irish folk to all corners of the globe, so it should be no surprise that this 'wanderlust' produces many very enthusiastic walkers in Ireland. Clubs abound and of recent years provision for walkers in the shape of footpaths and accommodation has reflected the growing enthusiasm.

Prominent among recent LDFP developments are the Wicklow Way south of Dublin, a proposed 'Ring of Kerry' round and including Ireland's highest mountain, Carrantuohill (1 040 m, 3 412 ft) in the south-west and the Ulster Way in the north. This last links Northern Ireland with Donegal in the Irish Republic and, like the European LDFPs, may well form a much wanted bond in a troubled land. Like the E-paths, too, it has a main route with circular tours and offshoots to villages and other paths as its principal features.

Elsewhere, paths may not always be much in evidence, but with the usual courtesies and common country-sense observed, you should have little difficulty in crossing open land as you please. If you do see someone and (of course) ask permission, you are more likely to be shown, after the traditional chat, the best way to go rather than be turned back.

Maps and guides

As Northern Ireland is part of the United Kingdom, it is covered by OS maps, but it does have its own office: the Ordnance Survey of Northern Ireland (OSNI) (see Useful Addresses). The OSNI is publishing a new series of 1:50 000 maps to replace the older one-inch maps and all the 18 sheets covering the whole country should be available in the near future. The Mourne Mountains are covered by a special 1:25 000 map and a very useful planning map at a scale of 1:250 000 entitled *Holiday Map, Northern Ireland* is also available.

Eire has its own Ordnance Survey Office (see Useful Addresses). The maps it publishes at scales of half-inch (1:126 720) and one-inch (1:63 360) that are normally useful to walkers need to be used with caution. Some have not been revised this century and, since the mountains were not considered important, they contain serious inaccuracies. A new corrected 1:50 000 series is planned but it will take a long time before maps covering the whole country are available. Careful compass work and good navigation skills will be needed in open country for a long time yet as a result.

Until recently, guides to walking in Ireland were not very numerous but the situation is now rapidly improving.

Guides to the Ulster Way and sections of it are available free from the Sports Council for Northern Ireland, and a guide to the Wicklow Way is available from Bord Fáilte, the Irish Tourist Board (see Useful Addresses).

A series of very comprehensive Irish Walk Guides, edited by Joss Lyman and published by Gill and Macmillan, cover the South-West, the West, North-West, East and South-East and are highly recommended.

The many walking and mountaineering clubs publish other guides: *Mountaineering in Ireland* from the Federation of Mountaineering Clubs of Ireland (FMCI) (see Useful Addresses) contains descriptions of many of the best walks, and *Dublin and the Wicklow Mountains* from the Irish Ramblers' Club can also be recommended.

Many others are now available in the equipment and larger bookshops.

Overnighting

Of most interest to walkers will be the family hotels, guesthouses, farms and private houses they will find on or near their route. 'Near' may have to be measured in Irish miles on occasion, so do check up before you book or plan your itinerary.

An Óige, the Irish Youth Hostels Association, has over 50 youth hostels well-placed for walking in Eire, and the Youth Hostels Association of Northern Ireland (YHANI) has 12 hostels useful to walkers. As elsewhere, the hostels vary from splendid old castles to simple huts and houses. Meals are not usually provided, but cooking and sleeping facilities are. Membership of a national YHA is of course necessary.

Camping is possible with the owner's permission almost anywhere in Ireland. Obviously, no one in his right mind would chance camping in a troubled area at the present time.

Recommended walking areas

From what has been said already, it is clear that the Mourne, Wicklow and Kerry mountains are the most popular areas. The West Coast has a very special atmosphere and remoteness all its own and spectacular cliff scenery. There is much to explore and discover almost everywhere else too.

Climate

'It isn't green for nothing' is a comment about Irish weather that many a wet-through walker has had cause to recall regretfully. As the first land-mass to meet Britain's prevailing wet south-west and west winds, Ireland does get considerable rainfall at almost any time of the year, but the gorgeous shades of green and the fine days more than make up for this.

Best times for walking are late spring and autumn.

Hazards

Snakes and mosquitoes are not hazards in Ireland, although other insects might be troublesome.

The terrain is not always easy and in the higher mountains must be treated with respect.

Delays due to prolonged passing of the time of day with people you meet will probably give you happy memories but problems with arriving on time. . . .

Language

Irish, a form of Gaelic, is spoken widely in Eire, but it is rare to meet anyone who does not or will not speak English.

Useful addresses

>Bord Fáilte (Irish Tourist Board)
>Baggot Street Bridge
>Dublin 2. Tel: (01) 765871

or (for postal enquiries)
>PO Box 273
>Dublin 8

or Irish Tourist Office
>590 Fifth Ave.
>New York, NY 10036 Tel: (212) 246-7400

for general information and some information on walking (Offices in Manchester, Birmingham and Glasgow also.)

>An Óige (Youth Hostel Association)
>39 Mountjoy Square South
>Dublin 1. Tel: (01) 745 734

for hostelling information and much else besides

Association for Adventure Sports (AFAS)
Tiglin Adventure Centre
Ashford
County Wicklow. Tel: (0404) 4169
for training courses and some walking information

Federation of Mountaineering Clubs of Ireland (FMCI)
21 Leopardstown Gardens
Black Rock
County Dublin
for much walking information and addresses of local clubs

Northern Ireland Tourist Board
River House
48 High Street
Belfast. Tel: (0232) 46609

for general information

Sports Council for Northern Ireland
49 Malone Road
Belfast BT9 6RZ. Tel: (0232) 663154
for information on Ulster Way

Youth Hostels Association of Northern Ireland (YHANI)
56 Bradbury Place
Belfast BT7 1RU. Tel: (0232) 24733
for hostelling information and much more

Chief Survey Officer
Department of the Environment
Ordnance Survey of Northern Ireland
83 Ladas Drive
Belfast. Tel: (0232) 701444

Assistant Director of Survey
Ordnance Survey
Phoenix Park
Dublin. Tel: (01) 213171
for maps

DENMARK

(DANMARK)

SINCE the abolition of censorship, Denmark has attracted attention for all the wrong reasons. Mention of the name conjures up an image of racy permissiveness, an image that is not at all appropriate, except in certain areas of the larger towns.

The better images are of Vikings and Hamlet's castle, the Little Mermaid and Danish bacon. Denmark is the only Scandinavian state attached to what may be called mainland Europe and is not one land-mass but a series of 400 islands, the main one being Zealand, on which stands the capital, Copenhagen.

Walking in Denmark

At present no organised network of long-distance paths exists in the country, although there is an extensive system of paths. A worthwhile exception to the rule is the traverse of Jutland, Funen and Zealand by European route E-6. There is also a plan to extend European route E-1 from Flensburg on the West German/Danish border up through Jutland to the Skagerrak coast.

Maps and guides

Within Denmark E-6 has been clearly waymarked by Landsforeningen Dansk Vanderlung (DLV). The markers are white crosses on specially erected posts or convenient trees. DLV have produced a set of three small guides to the route. The guides are brief, the route being shown on a section of 1:1 000 000 strip map with a key for towns and villages. Also listed are youth hostels, camp sites and hotels, transport and interesting sites.

The Danish Ordnance Survey publishes a 1:50 000 series of maps covering all the Danish islands. These are available throughout Denmark or through the Danish Tourist Board in Copenhagen (see Useful Addresses).

Overnighting

Denmark has an excellent hotel system with a full range of grades including budget accommodation, very useful to the walker. This includes self-catering holiday homes and farmhouse accommodation.

Camping is allowed in Denmark only at official sites, of which there are a large number, or with the landowner's permission. At official sites a Camping Carnet International is required, although a Danish camping pass can be purchased at the first site visited. Taking your own Carnet is cheaper and avoids problems on the first site.

There are some 90 youth hostels in Denmark which can be used to supplement the camp sites and hotels. Information on camp sites and hostels is available from Den Danske Lejpladsudvalg (see Useful Addresses).

Recommended walking areas

E-6 in Denmark is a worthwhile route as it requires the walker to use ferries to cross between the islands. These crossings, not always in the calmest of waters, turn walking trips into real adventures. The route also passes through

Roskilde with its museum of excavated Viking ships and cathedral with the tombs of Danish kings.

Also worthwhile is the Baltic coast of north-east Zealand.

Climate

The Danish climate is in the main temperate, but it can be very hot in midsummer (+30°C) because of strong easterly winds blowing for long periods. It can be very cold in winter (−30°C) for the same reason. Best times for walking are those avoiding these extremes, that is late spring/early summer or late summer/early autumn.

Hazards

None apart from those mentioned in the Introduction, unless you are prone to sea-sickness in which case the ferry crossings may not be too enjoyable.

Language

Danish is a Scandinavian language, said to be difficult for foreigners. This should not be too much of a problem as most Danes speak and/or understand English.

Useful addresses

> Danish Tourist Board
> 75 Rockefeller Plaza
> New York, NY 10019   Tel: (212) 582-2802

> Landsforeningen Dansk Vanderlung
> Kultorvet 7
> DK-1175 Kobenhavn K. Tel: (01) 12 11 65

Controls waymarking of the European route in Denmark (E-6) and can supply small guides to it with information on accommodation and transport.

Den Danske Lejpladsudvalg
Skjoldsgade 10
DK-2100 Kobenhavn O. Tel: (01) 42 32 22
for information on camp sites and youth hostels

Danmarks Touristrad
H.C. Andersens Boulevard 22
DK-1553 Kobenhavn V. Tel: (01) 13 70 07
for maps

FINLAND

(SUOMI = 'LAKELAND')

Ancient and mysterious they stand,
The Northland's dusky forests. . . .

SERIOUS music lovers will probably recognise these words which Sibelius, Finland's greatest composer, used to set the scene for his tone-poem, *Tapiola* – one of many depicting Finland in its wild, sometimes savage, remoteness. It is true that forest covers almost 70 per cent of Finland whilst over 60,000 lakes and tarns cover another 10 per cent of the land surface. North of the Arctic Circle, the forest gives way to an even harsher terrain of swamp, fell and low trees. Only on the coastal plain and the 30,000 islands to the south where the cities stand proud with their style-setting modern architecture, is there any softer agricultural countryside.

This might all seem forbidding and uninviting at first sight, but Finland affords walkers the chance to experience one of the last true great wilderness areas in Europe. For this reason alone, it is worthy of serious consideration.

Walking in Finland

With so much natural beauty to enjoy, the Finns are very dedicated to outdoor leisure activities. They tend also to be highly disciplined and sometimes authoritarian when they are out in their countryside. It should be no surprise therefore to find that, whilst they are very eager for you as a visitor to enjoy their splendid and very special natural environment, they will expect you to follow several regulations very carefully.

You are not allowed on private land without the owner's permission, for instance, nor in newly planted forest or crops. Breaking branches off living trees is forbidden, as is pulling up plants by the roots. Flowers, mushrooms and berries may be picked – except on private land and in Lapland. Litter is of course not to be thrown or left about, and birds, wild animals and reindeer herds are not to be disturbed. Above all, the lighting of fires except where expressly permitted by landowners or on special sites is forbidden in times of drought. But then with 70 per cent of their land as forest, who can blame the Finns for that?

In fact this apparently daunting array of 'don'ts' really reflects the very genuine concern of the Finns to conserve their environment and would, we hope, form part of any serious walker's make-up out anywhere in the countryside. If you do not subscribe to this concern, Finland is not for you. If you do, Finland offers you some of the greatest walking experiences possible in the whole of Europe.

To this end, the Finnish Government has created a system of footpaths that allow the visitor to see the country whilst protecting it from the consequences of mass onslaught. They are helped in this by the Suomen Matkailulutto (Finnish Travel Association) and the very active Suomen Latu (Finnish Ski-track Association) – see Useful Addresses. Both are voluntary associations which organise many hiking courses and activities, at some of which you would be very welcome – if you can grapple with their unbelievably difficult language! Most of the paths are in the southern and central parts of the country, but some LDFPs exist north of the Arctic Circle and on the northern borders of Sweden and

Norway. The paths vary in length and difficulty and are waymarked in different colours for different lengths so that it is possible to choose before setting out and then follow a particular colour all day or for several days. Apart from paint marks, wooden signposts are used and, unusual elsewhere, coloured plastic ribbon, often bright orange, is hung on trees to indicate the line to be followed.

Paths are not always easy to follow even so, and map and compass and experience in their use should be considered *essential* for walking anywhere in Finland.

Maps and guides

Maps exist in various scales. The 1:200 000 and 1:1 000 000 maps are intended to be used for 'basic planning' before you set out. On the trail you would be wise to use the larger-scale maps (1:20 000 or 1:50 000) as recommended in the many guides available for the route(s) you choose. Maps and guides are available from local tourist offices and hotels or from Maanmittanshallitus in Helsinki (see Useful Addresses).

Guides and the relevant maps for 'official' routes are most often sold together in an information pack, and the basic planning maps will usually give you a great deal of additional information about starting and finishing points, accommodation and places of interest *en route* etc. A very useful starter for route-planning is a booklet entitled *Finland – Hiking Routes* available free from the Finnish Tourist Board (see Useful Addresses). From this you would need to move on to the basic planning maps and/or the information packs.

The two voluntary associations mentioned on page 43 organise many tours, both summer and winter, and guides in (often very attractive) human form always lead them. Most of these guides speak at least one other language, often English, are very highly trained and are enthusiastic about their work.

Either association would be very happy to welcome you on their tours and would even organise a special one for you if you go as a sufficiently large group (12 or more).

Overnighting

In the towns and large villages, hotels of all grades exist, some of them of the highest modern standard and nearly all of them with the ubiquitous sauna. Out on the walking routes, however, accommodation can be sparse but very entertaining. It may be a private farmhouse where you can book a room in advance or, more often, a log cabin which may be quite lavishly equipped or simply a roof for the night.

A particular feature of Finnish accommodation is the holiday village or holiday cottage. The village usually consists of a large central building where you eat, take saunas and get together with fellow-walkers, and groups of cottages where you sleep. Nearly always these buildings will be log cabins or 'A'-houses, large or small and varying in standard from the spartan to those equipped with their own central heating, showers and saunas. These villages and cottages are listed in publications available from the national or local tourist offices and bookings need to be made in advance, especially in the holiday seasons, as they are very popular.

Camping is fairly rigidly controlled, but some 350 sites exist and are graded from one-star (simplest) to three-star. Here again, camp cabins and holiday cottages are available, so for centre-holidays a tent is not an absolute necessity.

Some 150 youth hostels exist in Finland, but most of them are only open in the summer. A one- to four-star system operates, there are no age restrictions and some have 'family rooms' which could be of interest to walking families.

Both the camp sites and hostels are listed in a brochure entitled *Camping & Youth Hostels* available free from the Finnish Tourist Board.

Recommended walking areas

'Anywhere and everywhere' is perhaps too obvious an answer to give, but in Finland it seems to be all too true. The major regions are:

The Coast and the Aland Islands are for gentle walking and visiting historic sites and little villages.

Finnish Lakeland – more central and to the north of Helsinki – is holiday cottage country par excellence. Good for mixed forest and lakeside walking.

Forest Finland – further north and east – is more remote and has several national parks where access is restricted and footpaths must be followed. Occasional bare hilltops rise above the forest lakes and rivers to give sweeping views over miles of unspoilt countryside.

Finnish Lapland – a very special experience. Wide expanses of open forest that give way to even greater expanses of open fells where only the tiny fell birch, sparse grasses, mosses and lichen eke out an existence. To be savoured – but not alone (see Hazards, below).

Climate

The Gulf Stream tempers the climate somewhat in summer, but Finland's northerly position means that winters are long (from October to May in the far north) and cold (down to −30°C).

North of the Arctic Circle, the Midnight Sun reigns from early June to early July with corresponding darkness (relieved by the glorious Northern Lights) from the end of November to early January.

Best times are therefore June and, because of the wonderful autumn colours, September–October.

Hazards

The only wild animals to fear are very tiny but occur in millions in July and August. They are called mosquitoes. Try to ignore them, take large amounts of insect-repellants if they work for you, or go at some other time if you can.

A more serious – and perhaps unforeseen – hazard is the nature of the terrain. 'Wilderness' means just that and the natural hazards of marsh, forest, river, lake and open fell are not to be taken lightly. Equipment needs to be considered carefully, footwear especially. Because it is most often wet under foot, the Finns wear rubber boots, at least calf-length, with cleated soles. You should do likewise – leather boots are *not* suitable. Most Finns will advise you – make you promise, even – *never to walk alone* in their wilderness areas. It is good advice almost anywhere but particularly so in such remote places. For the very experienced, walking alone in the wilderness can be one of the profoundest experiences on earth but it can be a very terrifying, even fatal, experience for anyone, experienced or not. *You have been warned!*

Language

The Finnish language almost defeats the Finns, so foreigners have problems! Fortunately, Swedish is the second language for all (it is easier) and many Finns speak German, English or French, sometimes all three. You will get by without too much difficulty in most tourist areas. Elsewhere, acting ability and sign language would be particularly useful.

Useful addresses

>Finland National Tourist Office
>75 Rockefeller Plaza
>New York, NY 10019   Tel: (212) 582-2802

Maanmittanshallitus
Kontamyynti
Ettläesplandi 10
SF-00130 Helsinki 13. Tel: (9)0 154 3105
for maps

Suomen Latu r.y. (Finnish Ski-track Association)
Fabianinkatu 7
SF-00130 Helsinki 13. Tel: (9)0 17 01 01.
the most active association for walkers and walking or cross-country skiing

Suomen Matkailulutto (Finnish Travel Association)
Mikonkatu 25
SF-00100 Helsinki 10. Tel: (9)0 17 08 68
for more general travel activities, holiday accommodation etc.

Suomen Retkeilymajajärjestö (Finnish Youth Hostels Association)
Yrjönkatu 38B
SF-00700 Helsinki 10. Tel: (9)0 694 0377
membership card from your own country necessary to use hostels

FRANCE

COBBLED village streets below splendid châteaux with old men drinking in cafés or playing *boules*, open spacious fields interspersed with rows of trees or woodland, or hills covered with vines as far as the eye can see, or hot sandy beaches covered with bronzing bodies under deep-blue skies – it is difficult to characterise France because it offers the visitor so much variety. It is also Europe's largest country after the USSR, and this contributes not only to the rich diversity of landscape but also to a sense of openness and space.

For the walker there are interesting and attractive possibilities everywhere. France can be said to 'slope upwards' towards the east and the south, and hill-walkers are understandably attracted towards the upland regions. The Pyrenees bordering Spain, the volcanic Massif Central a little to the north and east, the Vosges–Jura forming the frontiers with Germany and Switzerland and above all the French Alps with Western Europe's highest mountain, Mont Blanc (4 810 m, 15 780 ft), on the border with Italy – all offer exciting walking at all levels of difficulty. There are other regions too which are worth considering. Perhaps only the north of the Paris Basin (Picardy) is too flat to be very interesting, but Normandy has its 'Norman Switzerland', Brittany its rocky Armorican peninsula and its rugged coastline, and the centre has its valleys, gorges, wooded hills and châteaux. Add to these a fairly equable climate and there is little wonder that France is becoming an increasingly worthwhile country for the walker to visit.

Walking in France

La randonnée – 'hiking' or 'rambling' – has become a major French activity and part of the phenomenal growth in outdoor leisure activities that has swept France in the last twenty years. As a consequence and in order to make the most of their country's potential the French have 'trails' for canoeists, cyclists, horse-riders and walkers. The walkers' paths (*sentiers*) can be either *sentiers de petite randonnée* (SPR) offering about one day's walk or *sentiers de grande randonnée* (SGR) offering walks lasting several days and, since they interconnect, the possibility of traversing the whole of France. To date 30 000 km (19 000 miles) of SGR have been waymarked. They are of varying lengths. The GR 3, for instance, starts at Nantes, goes 350 km (220 miles) westward to Orléans, then south for a further 400 km (250 miles). In general, however, the SGRs are shorter – 100–200 km (60-120 miles) – but remember that because of interconnections from each end point longer walks are possible. Each route has a 'GR' number rather than being named and some of them are circular or can be planned in this way so that you can pick up your transport again when you finish.

The body responsible for the formation and upkeep of the *sentiers* and the encouragement of hiking in France is the Fédération Française de Randonnée Pédestre–Comité National de SGR (FFRP–CNSGR) – see Useful Addresses. This body divides the paths into different categories according to the condition of each path, the overnight accommodation and the amount of information available about them.

You will find most walkers on the paths in the July/August period and on the most popular – the all too well-known Tour du Mont Blanc, for instance – enough to form a veritable procession.

The paths are waymarked (*balisés*) by a red paint bar with a white one above and an occasional sign with the SGR number. Changes of direction are arrowed and wrong directions are marked with a red and white cross. All this is explained in much more detail in both maps and guides.

Maps and guides

At the top of the SGR category come those GRs for which a very detailed 'topo-guide' (from FFRP–CNSGR and sports and map shops) is available. This gives very full details of each section of the route, distances and times, villages and other points of interest *en route*, victualling and overnight possibilities, particular hazards and so on. Sectional maps based on the 1:50 000 Institut Géographique National (IGN) maps are interleaved so that the route can be traced out as you proceed.

Topo-guides for the SGRs which are not yet so fully provided for (i.e. the 'lower' categories) give as much information as is currently available. The most likely lack will be in accommodation, so camping is probably necessary.

Needless to say, if you intend to walk any SGR, its topo-guide is almost indispensable. You will also need maps since those in the guides are not really adequate.

Maps come from several sources, the principal Ordnance Survey equivalent being published by the IGN. Its main series are:

Rouge (red) 16 sheets covering France (scale - 1:250 000)
Verte (green) 74 sheets at 1:100 000
Orange 1100 sheets at 1:50 000
Bleue (blue) 2000 sheets at 1:25 000

Special maps cover particular areas; for example, mountain regions and forests at 1:25 000, and regional and national parks (1:50 000 and 1:100 000). IGN also publishes Sheet 903, *Sentiers de Grande Randonnée*, at 1:1 000 000, showing all the LDFPs and the waymarking system with a key in English and German.

Other maps for particularly popular areas exist and come from a variety of sources. Local tourist offices are the best place to start if you want any of these.

Overnighting

France has hotels, of course, in abundance and at all categories. A national star system from 1 (simple grade) to 4 (luxury) exists and for walkers one and two star hotels are usually adequate. In the remoter areas they may indeed be the only ones available. The price of a room is displayed in the foyer and in the room itself. Breakfast (*petit déjeuner*) is sometimes included, sometimes not, so always ask.

In addition to hotels, many SGRs have *Gîtes d'étape*, sometimes in a continuous chain along them. *Gîtes* vary, but are essentially simple accommodation where walkers can wash, eat and sleep, often in dormitories. Cooking facilities are provided and when the *gîte* is part of a farm, or specially built and wardened, simple but very wholesome meals are available. The *gîte* system is rapidly developing as a life-saver to many rural economies in France and you will be well advised to try them. They are almost certain to add a very French touch to your holiday, even if they cost a little more than camping.

Camping in France is very well provided for, almost every town and village of any note having its *terrain de camping municipal*. In the popular tourist areas very highly organised camp sites abound, but they are often full in high season, so booking is necessary. Farmers will usually give permission (and fresh farm produce) for a single night's camping –

perhaps more. And in the remoter areas, all that is required is the ability to be up and away early in the morning!

Recommended walking areas

Almost every area has its possibilities and rarely is an SGR far away. As indicated already, the north is probably the least attractive, although GR 12, 121 and 122 are all north of Paris.

Paris has a network of SGRs which run around its outer perimeter, mostly through its famous *bois* and *forêts*.

Western France – La Suisse Normande (GR 36), Armorican Peninsula (GR 34 and 37 west of Rennes). Périgord (GR 36)

Central France – Loire Valley (GR 3, Orléans–Tours etc.), Burgundy–Beaujolais Lyonnais (GR 7), Morvan (GR 13), Massif Central (GR 4), Cévennes (GR 6 and a very dense network of branching paths); Aquitaine (GR 65) is an old pilgrimage route to St James of Compostella in Spain.

Eastern France – Vosges (GR 5/E-2 south-east of Strasbourg), Jura (GR 5/E-2 continues to Geneva).

Pyrenees – GR 10 traverses the range from the Atlantic to the Mediterranean. The National Park in the centre, around Gavarnie, is particularly fine.

Alps – Almost endless possibilities. Very popular but worthwhile are: the Tour du Mont Blanc (TMB) and the GR 5 (E-2) from Lake Geneva to Nice. Growing in popularity are: the Écrins National Park (GR 54), the Vercors (GR 91-94) and the Queyras (GR 5 and 58B). The information centre CIMES in the Maison du Tourisme, Grenoble, is a goldmine for the Alps and most other upland areas of France.

Corsica – the GR 20 traverses the island. Very rugged and sometimes very remote, it is really *for experienced walkers only*. French alpinists have been known to give up, so go prepared and take care.

Coastal paths – exist in many areas in varying degrees of *balisage*. The French aim to have a footpath right round their coastline, but this may remain a pipe-dream for a very long time yet.

Climate

Climate varies greatly from north to south. The northern coastal areas are temperate. Further inland the climate becomes more 'continental' with hotter summers and colder, drier winters. Eastern France is prone to sultry weather with thunderstorms in July and August, while rain, and snow, occur further south and, of course, with increasing altitude. The Pyrenees have the reputation of being very sunny and hot, but late August is often wet. The Mediterranean areas are the hottest – May, June, September and October are best for walkers.

Hazards

Drinking water used to be suspect but is less so now in most parts of France. Beware the *eau non potable* sign and always ask if in doubt. See remarks regarding snakes and rabies in the Introduction.

Useful addresses

> French Government Tourist Office
> 610 Fifth Ave.
> New York, NY 10020   Tel: (212) 757-1125
>
> Monaco Consulate
> 20 E. 49th St.
> New York, NY 10017   Tel: (212) 759-5227

Monaco is at one end of GR 52.

Club Pirinenc Andorra
Carrer de l'Unio 2
Andorra la Vella
Principat d'Andorra

Andorra is crossed by a branch of GR 10.

FFRP–CNSGR
92 rue de Clignancourt
75883 Paris CEDEX 1. Tel: (1) 259 60 40

for topo-guides and some maps and up-to-date information on footpaths

IGN
107 rue La Boétie
75008 Paris. Tel: (1) 225 87 90

for 'official' maps

Michelin Guides, including *Camping in France*, for most popular areas are available in English from bookshops.

Touring Club de France
Comité Pédestre
65 Avenue de la Grande Armée
75782 Paris. Tel: (1) 532 22 15

Fédération Française des Auberges de la Jeunesse
12 rue des Barres
Paris 4

Club Alpin Français
7 rue La Boétie
75008 Paris. Tel: (1) 265 54 45

GREECE

(HELLAS)

For anyone who is European in origin or has a sense of Europe, Greece holds a very special interest. Justly claiming to be 'the cradle of European civilisation' (including the very name itself), it has been able to profit from its classical past and develop tourism as a major industry. Its thousands of historic sites and remains, its hot, sunny climate and its cheerful people have all attracted more and more tourists to it every year.

Anyone who has been to Greece or has seen pictures of it knows that it is essentially a hilly country with rocky terrain that pushes out into the sea, scattering into some 500 equally rocky islands in its archipelago. In fact nearly 80 per cent of Greece can be considered mountainous, and in addition to its most famous and highest mountain, Mount Olympus (2 917 m, 9 568 ft), it has more than eighty summits over 2 000 m (6 500 ft) high.

All this should bode well for walkers, especially those with an interest in archaeology or ancient history. Unfortunately this is not yet the case, although there are signs that the Greeks are beginning to realise the tourist potential of their mountain areas, especially for skiing.

Walking in Greece

There are countless tracks on the mountains, but few of them are waymarked and there are no official, designated long-distance routes. The paths that are marked are local and usually lead up to a particular summit and back. Route-finding off the paths can be difficult and there is a paucity of sufficiently good maps. Furthermore, any notions of 'the freedom to roam' might not be easily understood, especially on the borders with Eastern Europe, Albania and Bulgaria in particular, where it would be very ill-advised. Finally the nature of the terrain itself, rocky or scrub-covered, can present obstacles that could deter all but the most experienced walker/mountaineer.

For this last, the Greek mountains have more to offer. The one organisation that seems at all concerned with mountain-travel is the Hellenic Federation of Mountaineering and Skiing (see Useful Addresses). As its name implies, it is more interested in climbing as such rather than walking but some of the information it publishes could be useful to the walker capable of extending himself to climbing at lower grades. It is the Federation's local groups that are responsible for waymarking whatever routes exist on their local mountains.

Greece then is still very much for experienced walkers in search of true adventure and with a real ability to pioneer their route as they go.

Maps and guides

The paucity of really good maps has already been mentioned. They are only available from the National Survey Service (see Useful Addresses) and at a scale of 1:200 000 – hardly sufficient for detailed route-finding. Guides in published form are not generally available, but the local mountaineering club may be able to provide you with a sketch map and a short (verbal) description of the route. The HFMS also has a small library in Athens.

Overnighting

In its present tourist resorts, Greece now has some of the most modern hotels in Europe. Indeed they come in no less than six categories: Luxury, A, B, C, D and E followed on the lists by 'Inns'. In the mountains, these last may well be the only form of accommodation available for the walker. They will vary in quality.

Higher up on the most popular mountains, HFMS is rapidly implanting mountain refuges. Many now exist in various shapes and sizes, some wardened and offering meals and hot showers, others much simpler. All offer water, cooking and sleeping facilities.

Camping is allowed on official sites only and the Greek publications warn you that 'Freelance camping is not allowed in any part of the country'.

Recommended walking areas

It is difficult in these circumstances to make particular recommendations. Obviously, the best-known peaks, Olympus, Parnassus, Pelion, would be on the list. Northern Greece might be the most enjoyable if only because it is often (marginally) cooler.

Climate

'Hot, dry summers, warm, wet winters' is an old tag that can really apply in Greece. It can be very hot in the height of summer (28°C average in July) but the mountains are a little cooler, and in winter snow can be found above 1 800 m (5 900 ft), allowing the Greeks to develop skiing as a tourist attraction.

Best times to go are late spring or early summer – or for the winter sports.

Hazards

The common Mediterranean ones: snakes, rabies etc. (see Introduction) and the consequences of great heat if you suffer from them. The Greeks claim that bears, wolves, even jackals live in their mountains. You are highly unlikely to meet any of them, still less to be attacked by them. Scorpions can be a particular hazard in some areas.

Water can be a hazard. Springs in the mountains (up to 2 000 m, 6 500 ft) should be all right, but boil or purify anything at all suspect anywhere else.

Language

Difficulties can be considerable outside the main resorts. Vaguely remembered ancient Greek will not help much – good acting and goodwill should help a lot.

Useful addresses

>Greek National Tourist Office
>645 Fifth Ave.
>New York, NY 10022   Tel: (212) 421-5777

or National Tourist Organisation of Greece
>Information Department
>2 Amerikis Street
>Athens 133. Tel: (1) 3223111-9,

for more information and cyclostyled sheets entitled 'Mountaineering and Skiing in Greece' for the fullest information available

Otherwise
>The Hellenic Federation of Mountaineering and Skiing
>7 Karageorgi Servias
>Athens 126. Tel: (1) 3234555

and
>National Survey Service
>14 str, Lykourgou
>Athens.

HOLLAND

(NEEDERLANDE)

TULIP fields and clogs, dykes and windmills are the correct images of Holland. The almost uniformly flat countryside makes long-distance walking a somewhat unrewarding experience, but shorter walks, centre-based, can be worthwhile and walkers with other interests, history or bird-watching for instance, will find it very rewarding indeed.

Walking in Holland

Despite the almost level terrain, the Dutch themselves are very enthusiastic walkers (usually in other countries!). Sections of LDFPs from other countries and a branch of the E-2 path exist. Local groups have also produced a system of footpaths throughout the country. These groups have been brought together under a single umbrella organisation – Stichting Lange-afstand-Wandelen (LAW) – which, in conjunction with the Royal Dutch Touring Club (ANWB), now speak with a single voice on future prospects (see Useful Addresses). However, for the present system of some 30 routes the situation is largely piecemeal. The routes vary in length from 50 to 300 km (30-190 miles); they average about 100 km (60 miles). They also vary in the amount of information available on them. Many have no waymarking (*geen markering*), while others are well marked with a variety of different symbols, orange Hs, wooden stakes etc. Such markings are consistent, however, and avoid confusion where routes cross.

Maps and guides

Guides exist for the majority of the LDFPs, though they are not of uniform quality. The waymarked routes tend to have topo-guides with map extracts and notes on the countryside and accommodation, while some of the non-marked paths have guides without maps, although the maps required for the route are noted. This can be very awkward if the guide is written for a single direction of travel only. Before buying such a guide, and remember they are only available in Dutch, check to see if it is *alleen in vermelde richting*, only in the stated direction, or *in twee richting*, a two-way guide.

The Dutch Ordnance Survey – Topografische Dienst – publishes surveys at scales of 1:10 000, 1:25 000, 1:50 000 and larger-scale maps.

The Dutch Survey is possibly unique in offering a series that does not include contours. Since the land is so flat, contours and spot heights are required only for water control, and contoured maps – *Hoogtekaart* – are available for that purpose, at an extra price.

LAW, in conjunction with ANWB, publish a 1:5 000 000, the *Wandelroutekaart*, map of Holland with the trail network marked on it. The map descriptions are in Dutch.

Overnighting

Holland has an excellent hotel system with hotels at all grades, including budget accommodation for the walker.

There is an extensive system of camp sites, all with good facilities, but the walker's 'best buy' is, possibly, the Dutch Youth Hostel system with some 50 hostels strategically placed. Membership of your own national YHA is necessary before you use them, of course.

Recommended walking areas

No one area stands out, because of the uniformity of the country. However, the North Sea coast and Zuyder Zee, north of Amsterdam, are of interest to the ornithologist-walker, while the interior, north-east of Utrecht and north of Arnhem, has some excellent woodland areas and river valleys.

Climate

Holland has a marine-type climate: cool summers and comparatively mild winters. Winter frosts can be severe enough to freeze the canals, however (skating is a national pastime), and summer can be wet.

Best seasons for walking are late spring, when the flowers are out, and summer.

Hazards

None, other than those mentioned in the Introduction except perhaps the unusual possibility of being run down by a bicycle!

Language

Words like *Biefstuk* on a menu, *Let op*! at a road junction or a shout of *Komm on*! in the street make Dutch a tantalising language for English-speakers. If you also have some German, it will be even more intriguing. With no language flair at all, however, you have no need to worry: English is the first foreign language in the schools so there are very few Dutch who do not understand it and most speak it very well.

Useful addresses

>Netherlands Tourist Office
>576 Fifth Ave.
>New York, NY 10036   Tel: (212) 245-5320

or Bozuidenhoutseweg 2,
>N-2954 AV
>Den Haag. Tel: (70) 814191

or simply VVV
>Town you wish to visit
>Holland.

>Stichting Lange-afstand-Wandelen
>P.C. Hoofstraat 163
>1071 BV Amsterdam. Tel: (20) 766889.

>ANWB (Royal Dutch Touring Club)
>Wassenaatseweg 220
>2596 EC 'S Gravenhage. Tel: (70) 636968

for the Wandelroutekaart, *showing the LDFP network and giving the Dutch addresses from which information on the individual routes can be obtained*

>Stichting Nederlandse Jeugdherberg Centrale (NJHC)
>Prof. Tulpplein 4
>1018 GX Amsterdam. Tel: (20) 264433

for information on Dutch youth hostels

>Grote Routepaden
>Van Stralenstraat 40
>2000 Antwerpen
>Belgium. Tel: (31) 232 72 18

for topo-guides for the Dutch sections of Franco-Belgian SGRs, in Dutch

ICELAND

(ISLAND)

MANY countries have been mis-named in history, but Iceland, so named by Viking explorers some eleven hundred years ago, must be near the top of the league for misnomers. Ice there is: the country lays claim to the world's largest glacier outside the polar regions; but it is also one of the world's hot-spots. Volcanic activity is fairly continuous with new islands sometimes appearing or villages being destroyed in a few months by eruptions and lava flows. In some parts, hot springs abound: the very word 'geyser' comes from the area of Geysir in the south-west of the island. Iceland is inevitably a land of dramatic contrasts, a land of 'ice and fire' as the publicity brochures rightly claim. Geographers may regard it as a 'barren outpost of Europe' set in the Atlantic Ocean just south of the Arctic Circle, but walkers find it a world rich in its variety of rolling plateaux, studded with lakes and tarns, sculpted basalt pillars, jagged ridges and ice-capped peaks. It is also rich in challenge and adventure for walkers who are prepared to accept the hardships these often bring with them.

Walking in Iceland

With its population of some 250,000 concentrated largely in settlements round the coast, Iceland has an interior almost totally devoid of inhabitants. A rudimentary road system was much extended by American and British troops during the

Second World War, but outside the towns these roads are still mostly gravel or dirt. Footpaths hardly exist at all so that walking across open land is very much the norm. So are daily stream or river crossings, and if you do not have webbed feet before you start, you probably will have when you have finished a trek into the interior!

Most 'expeditions' are taken by specialist tour operators who use Jeeps or Land Rovers to transport gear and food part of the way, but you must be prepared for back-packing beyond a certain point if you really wish to explore the country. It is essentially hostile and is *not* for the inexperienced. The penalties for accidents and mistakes in navigation are likely to be extreme.

Maps and guides

A series of maps exists at various scales from a 1:1 000 000 map of the whole island to a few 1:25 000 maps of certain areas. Particularly recommended for walkers are the main touring maps at 1:250 000 which show surprisingly good detail, the 1:100 000 maps and, for the south and west, the 1:50 000 maps (Myvatn in the north also has a special sheet at this scale).

The real problem with maps for Iceland is that some have not been revised since before the Second World War and some are out of print. In a country where the terrain is constantly changing because of so much geological activity, this is not the happiest state of affairs. The best advice is to use the 1:1 000 000 map for planning and then to buy on the spot or from one of the specialist tour operators (see Useful Addresses).

Not surprisingly, Iceland, so exciting to geographers, geologists and mountaineers, has been the subject of many books, apart from producing its own famed and ancient sagas and eddas. The best for starters is *Iceland in a Nutshell* by Peter Kidson. Also useful if you want to know more or get 'hooked' is the *Check-list of Principal Books on Iceland and Faroe* by Dick Phillips (see Useful Addresses) which lists some 300 books in English and even then excludes Viking and saga material.

Overnighting

Hotels from luxury to 'economy' grade exist in the major centres. Simpler and more spartan accommodation is to be found elsewhere on occasion.

Youth hostels are an important feature of the accommodation provided for walkers. They vary from the one in Reykjavik with bathrooms and hot showers to simple, isolated but very welcome turf houses in the interior. Membership of a national YHA would be useful but is not essential.

Camping is allowed outside the cities and villages anywhere that is suitable, except for cultivated or fenced-in areas. Some special camp sites exist but facilities vary and could be very simple indeed. In some parts, of course, camping is the only option available.

Recommended walking areas

In its 100,000 square kilometres, Iceland still has some areas almost unexplored, but most walkers will want to see the hot springs areas (if only for a welcome bath) and the ice-caps. Most of the organised tours include some of each (see Useful Addresses).

Climate

Perhaps a little surprisingly, Iceland has cool summers and mild winters, the first because of its latitude, the second because of the Gulf Stream. Snow in winter and rain at other times is brought by the south-west winds, so that more falls in the south of the island than in the north.

Hazards

In a word – terrain. As already stated, Iceland is not a place for the ill-prepared or the inexperienced, and is certainly not a place for going it alone. 'Uninhabited country' really means what it says in Iceland: you have been warned. . . .

Language

English is taught in all the schools so most people in the inhabited areas understand and/or speak English. Elsewhere, you may have difficulty, but that will probably be in meeting and speaking to anybody at all in any language!

Useful addresses

>Icelandic National Tourist Office
>75 Rockefeller Plaza
>New York, NY 10026
>Tel: (212) 582-2802

for maps, guides and much else besides including organised tours

>Icelandic Tourist Board
>3 Laugavegur
>Reykjavik

or Outdoor Life Tours
Laekjargata #6A
Reykjavik

Also useful for organised walking tours are:
Touring Club of Iceland
Öldudötu #3
Reykjavik

ITALY

(ITALIA)

PIZZA and pasta, operatic tenors and rough red wine, old hilltop cities where every turning provides yet another film set – all these and many other images crowd into the tourist's experience of Italy. Walkers can also come away with similar impressions but, if they choose wisely, much more as well. In the north, the continuation of the Alps south over the French, Swiss and Austrian borders ensures fine walking opportunities, with the added bonus of more sunshine generally than is the case 'on the other (that is the northern) side'. Snow and ice scenery that is typically 'Alpine' abounds, but the very special glory of the Italian Alps is the Dolomites. Great walls of rock towering vertically for thousands of feet above flower-filled valleys make for some of the most dramatic scenery to be found in Europe – a veritable paradise for walkers. Further south, as far as Rome, the long spine of the Apennines offers gentler but still demanding walking and no walker worth his or her salt would miss the chance, if given it, of visiting Vesuvius, south of Naples, or Etna in Sicily.

Apart from all this, the constant reminders of Italy's historic role in Europe, the cheerful friendliness of the Italians and their ready welcome to visitors put Italy firmly on the map for walking abroad.

Walking in Italy

The all-too-familiar pear or barrel shape associated with the film image of Italians might suggest that they are more likely to roll round on an outing than walk. In fact, many Italians are very keen walkers as a visit to their very crowded mountains in *Feragosto* – the August holiday – will quickly show.

The main focus of activity, not unexpectedly, is the north, and the national walking organisation, the Federazione Italiana Escursionismo (FIE) has its headquarters in Turin (see Useful Addresses). Nine regional committees promote walking interests all over the country and the FIE collaborates with other organisations, notably the Club Alpino Italiano (CAI) and the Touring Club Italiano (TCI), in developing the footpath network.

Two European LDFPs have terminal (or starting) points in Italy: the E-1 in Pegli, near Genoa – with an extension planned to La Spezia – and the E-5 in Venice. The Italians have been very enthusiastic supporters of European LDFPs and have done much to waymark and maintain their sections of them.

Elsewhere, the maintenance and waymarking of paths varies a great deal.

In the less popular walking regions, some parts of the Apennines for instance, footpaths are not always easy to follow. Tourism and technology have not been a happy blend for footpaths here. Most tourists who visit the region do so by car and are more interested in aspects of tourism other than walking. The Italian inhabitants of the area, too, are mostly car-owners so that old mule-tracks which connected one hill-village with another and would have formed an ideal, almost idyllic, network for walkers are now hot and fume-ridden metalled roads or have quite simply disappeared in tangled undergrowth through lack of use. The FIE and local Ente Provinciale (tourist offices), aware of the tourist potential of such paths, are trying to do something about it, but it may be too late. This is a great pity, since many of these areas offer splendid walking possibilities. Do make careful enquiries before you plan a walking holiday in them.

In the high mountains further north, however, the picture is very different. Here footpaths abound, are usually well maintained, waymarked and numbered, and offer walkers all levels of strenuousness.

Of particular interest are the *alte vie* (high routes) which are more and more in evidence in the Alps and the Dolomites. As their name suggests, they are paths which stay high, contouring round valley heads or traversing from valley to valley, as close as possible to the highest peaks without demanding too much mountaineering expertise. Staging posts in the form of *rifugi* (mountain huts) or other forms of accommodation exist or are planned along them and they offer walkers some of the best experience of 'middle mountain' possible anywhere. Red, white, or yellow triangles with a number in them indicate that you are on such a path and yellow signs with altitudes, times and other path numbers to various destinations will help you *en route*. As these paths are still comparatively new in some places, the way ahead may not always be clear. These sections are shown on maps or in the guides and you should be prepared to use map and compass on them.

If the waymarking colour changes to red, and especially if the waymark is a red star, pause and consider. These paths are Alpine Club paths and may well lead you into difficult spots. If the path is already hard for you, turn back, for it is likely to get harder, especially beyond the red star. These are the *vie attrezzatte*, 'equipped' paths, where the 'equipment' is going to be fixed ropes, iron rungs or ladders, and an essential bit of personal equipment will be a good head for heights. Walkers with scrambling/rock-climbing experience will find them a delight, others may well find them a nightmare. They will find a multitude of other paths to give them pleasure elsewhere. In the Dolomites, a further extension of the *vie attrezzate* exists in the shape of the *vie ferrate*. These 'iron shod' routes lead to even more dramatic and airy situations high across the vertical rock-walls and should only be attempted by those with very good and long experience of rock-climbing and extended scrambling. They are *not* for the average walker and *definitely not* for the beginner.

Maps and guides

Ordnance Survey type maps of Italy at scales of 1:25 000 and 1:100 000 are published by the Instituto Geografico Militare and a 1:50 000 series is published by the Istituto Geografico Centrale and the Touring Club Italiano (see Useful Addresses).

Also of interest to walkers are maps from other publishers. Much of the alpine region of Italy used to be the Austrian South Tyrol, so it is not surprising to find that the Freytag-Berndt 1:100 000 series covers these areas fully. Kompass walking maps (*Carte Turistiche*) at 1:50 000 are also available for the most popular areas and an Italian publisher, Casa Editrice Tabacco, produces similar maps at the same scale.

As with other parts of the Alps, the best advice is to start your planning with the 1:100 000 Freytag-Berndt map and buy the larger-scale maps on the spot. In this way, you make sure of the greatest and most up-to-date choice.

Guidebooks come in a bewildering variety.

The Club Alpino Italiano (CAI) is publishing guides in a series called 'Guida dei Monti d'Italia' planned to cover all the Italian mountain regions including Sardinia. Some 30 of the 49 planned are now available, but they exist only in Italian and are really for alpinists. CAI also publish guides to particular areas for walkers. These need to be sought out on the spot, and again are in Italian.

Guides to some of the *alte vie* in the Dolomites and the Alps are available from local tourist offices and some of them are in English.

Yet again, the best advice is to wait until you are in the area before you buy and always start at the local tourist office.

Overnighting

As perhaps the leading tourist nation in Europe, Italy has developed a highly organised system of accommodation for tourists. Lists showing hotels in four classes, pensions in three and inns (unclassified), together with officially agreed prices for services offered, exist everywhere. The lists are of course available in the ubiquitous Ente Provinciale per il Turismo or Azziendadi Soggiorno – the local tourist offices. What is more, these offices will usually try, move heaven and earth even, to find you accommodation at the price you choose. For walkers on tour, such a service is invaluable, and the very first call if you arrive without accommodation in a village after a long tiring day should be the tourist office. Almost invariably someone speaks English or French and seems to have the ear of room-providers for up to 50 km (30 miles) around. Best of all, the service is free or costs very little. You may finish up in what looks like a *mafioso* hideout, but even if it is, it will be clean and often provide splendid Italian cuisine into the bargain!

The CAI mountain huts – *rifugi* – vary in size and services from the simple *bivacco* for use in emergency high in the mountains to the elaborate *alberghetto* on the roadside. This last is very similar to the Austrian huts and a considerable network of them some 5 or 6 hours apart exist in almost every part of the Italian Alps. Membership of an alpine club (most have reciprocal rights for use of each other's huts) will save you money if you are going to use them at all frequently on tour. Some privately-owned huts also exist.

Camping sites in apparently endless numbers (over 1600, in fact) seem to exist everywhere in Italy, and the popular spots will certainly have more than one site with at least basic facilities and most often much more. They may not be of much use to you if you are on an *alta via*, but they make very satisfactory bases for walks from centres.

Youth hostels also exist in Italy, but they do not form satisfactory link-ups for walkers on tour.

Finally, there are villas, flats and chalets available for renting at most centres, and through 'Agriturist' (see Useful Addresses) it is possible to rent a cottage or farmhouse for a holiday.

Remember, the place to start is *always* the tourist office!

Recommended walking areas

Enough has probably been said above to indicate a distinct leaning towards the north of Italy. Outside the big cities, it is possible to find good walking almost anywhere. Walkers with a special interest in nature – most, we hope – would do well to visit either the Gran Paradiso National Park, near Aosta on the French border, or the Stelvio National Park, near Bormio, on the Austrian border.

Further south, the Ligurian and Tuscan Apennines have interesting possibilities and are rapidly developing their walking potential. Further south still, the heat at usual summer holiday times begins to be a major factor and an obstacle to serious walking.

Climate

So far south in Europe, hotter, sunnier weather is usually to be expected. Many walkers wet through and fed up have crossed the north–south divide of the Alps to find blue skies and to dry out! Even so, it can rain, and sudden, quite violent thunderstorms and snow do occur on occasion. In prolonged periods of fine weather, great heat can be too much for some, and this can last well into September.

Despite this, the best times for walking are mid-June to mid-September (but remember *Feragosto* mentioned on p. 70).

Hazards

Snakes are mentioned constantly in Italian writings about walking areas and they recommend carrying an anti-snake-bite kit at all times. In many years' experience, we have yet to see a single poisonous snake – but you have been warned!

Otherwise the hazards are as in the Introduction.

Language difficulties

For anyone with a smattering of any Romance language, Italian is not difficult to understand if it is read. When it is spoken by a highly excitable or excited Italian (most of them) its sheer rapidity may well defeat you. Try French, especially in the Aosta and Genoese areas, or English. This last will most often promote a very warm response and sometimes very surprising English as well.

Useful addresses

    Italian Government Travel Office
    630 Fifth Ave.
    New York, NY 10020   Tel: (212) 245-4822
Tell them where you are going and what you hope to do.

In Italy:
Ente Provinciale per il Turismo (EPT) (Regional Tourist Office) in the large town or city nearest your destination. *Over 400 Local Tourist Boards look after local information, so try the Azzienda di Soggiorno in the town or village you intend to visit.*

>EPT
>Via r. Psara 21
>32100 Belluno. Tel: (437) 22043

for the Dolomite alte vie

>Federazione Italiana Escursionismo (FIE)
>Via Cibrario 33
>10143 Torino Tel: (11) 740 011

or Club Alpino Italiano (CAI)
>Via Ugo Foscolo 3
>Milano. Tel: (2) 80 25 54

for information on LDFPs, walking activities etc.

>Touring Club Italiano (TCI)
>Curso Italia
>10 Milano. Tel: (2) 80 98 71

for mountain huts, guidebooks and maps, camping-list

>Casa Editrice Tabacco
>Via della Rosta 15
>Udine Tel: (432) 21943

>Kompass Carte Turistiche
>S.a.r.l. Instituto Geografico
>Via Dante 10
>Bolzano

for maps

>Agriturist
>Corso V. Emanuele 101
>Roma. Tel: (6) 656 4242

for cottages and farmhouses

Centro Nazionale Campeggiatori Stranieri
Casella Postale 649
50100 Firenze
for camping information

Associazione Italiana Alberghi per la Gioventù
Palazzo della Civiltà del Lavoro
Quadrato della Concordia
00144 E.U.R. Roma. Tel: (6) 591 3702
for youth hostels

LIECHTENSTEIN

(FÜRSTENTUM LIECHTENSTEIN)

VAGUE notions of a somewhat run-down Ruritanian state will be dispelled as soon as you set foot in Liechtenstein. It may be one of the smallest European states (some 160 square kilometres – 60 square miles) but it is modern and outward-looking and well aware of its potential for tourism.

Walkers will not find much of interest on its western flank where the Rhine alluvial plain forms the border with Switzerland, although footpaths exist; but eastwards, towards Austria, the foothills of the Rätikon Alps rise rapidly to over 2 000 m (6 500 ft). If you care to stop off, then, in Liechtenstein you will not be disappointed.

Walking in Liechtenstein

The eleven communities that make up the principality claim with good reason one of the densest footpath networks in Europe. The footpaths may be short by LDFP standards, although part of the Austrian Zentralalpenweg passes through Liechtenstein, but by judicious choosing you will be able to find routes that give what many walkers consider the best of all mountain experiences: high-level ridge walking. In addition to these high-level paths (*Bergrouten*) Liechtenstein offers a host of lower-level field and forest paths (*Feld-* and *Waldwege*). These latter paths are so well maintained and waymarked that even very modest walkers should have no difficulty in finding their way on them. They include historic paths and nature trails and vary in the time needed to complete them from 30 minutes to 4 hours.

The high-level paths present one or two local difficulties, but nothing that an experienced walker cannot cope with or circumvent.

Maps and guides

A single map at a scale of 1:50 000 covers the country and the Liechtenstein Government produces one. It shows all the waymarked paths. Some of the communities also produce local maps.

A 1:50 000 map is produced by Agfa, the film makers, designed primarily to show the best viewpoints for taking pictures. There is also a Freytag-Berndt 1:100 000 map of the Silvretta–Verwall mountain groups that includes Liechtenstein. This map is useful if you are planning to use hut-to-hut routes. A sketch map, *Vaduz und Umgebung*, showing walks round Vaduz is available from the Tourist Office.

A guide to all the routes in the principality is published by Fink-Kümmerly and Frey. It is Guide No. 5 of the *International Reihe* (International Series) entitled *Fürstentum Liechtenstein* (in German only) and is available from the publisher or from the Fremdenverkehrszentrale in Liechtenstein itself – as are the maps mentioned above (see Useful Addresses). This guide contains details of some 85 low-level and 15 high-level routes.

A guidebook *Excursions in the Principality of Liechtenstein* (in English) may be available in Vaduz. It details some 80 walks.

Overnighting

Hotels well up to international standards offer high levels of comfort and service. There are also *Privatzimmer* and *Zimmer zu vermieten* (rooms in private houses). In the mountains the Liechtensteiner Alpenverein (LAV – Alpine Club), which is responsible for the upkeep of the paths, runs a small number of huts with reciprocal rights for members of other alpine clubs and there are also a number of privately owned huts.

There are three camping sites and a youth hostel.

Recommended walking areas

North-east of Vaduz lies the Drei Schwesterngruppe (Three Sisters Group). A splendid ridge path runs along it from the LAV hut Gafadura to the village of Steg. It includes the famous Fürstensteig (Prince's Step), an airy *mauvais pas* where a good head for heights is needed. Fixed ropes or an easier way round help the insecure.

On the southern border the Naafkopf (2 570 m, 8 430 ft), the second highest peak, can be climbed from the LAV's Pfälzerhutte. From here, too, it is possible to continue into Austria and on to the main ridge of the Rätikon group and its main peak, Scesaplana (2 765 m, 9 725 ft), a very easy snow summit.

From almost any spot in Liechtenstein, a comprehensive bus service enables you to start and finish your walks wherever you please. There is no lack of choice.

Climate

Because of its sheltered position, Liechtenstein has a relatively mild climate, but remember that in the Alps, rain, snow and thunderstorms can occur at any time.

Good in all summer months for walking, best outside the high season.

Hazards

None beyond the usual ones mentioned in the Introduction, except perhaps the temptation to overspend in Vaduz. The Liechtensteiners will not mind!

Language

German is the principal language. You will find many who speak English as well.

Useful addresses

>Liechtensteinische Fremdenverkehrszentrale
>(Tourist Office)
>Städtele 37
>POB 139
>FL-9490 Vaduz. Tel: (75) 2 14 43 or 6 62 88

>Swiss National Tourist Office
>608 Fifth Ave.
>New York, NY 10020 Tel: (212) 757-5944

>Liechtensteiner Alpenverein (LAV)
>Ramschwagweg
>FL-9496 Balzers. Tel: (75) 4 12 49

for mountain hut details

LUXEMBOURG

A HAZY recollection of winding river valleys and wooded hills topped by an occasional château, something that happened between Belgium and Germany, may well be all that the traveller on wheels retains of Luxembourg. Hardly surprising, since this tiny country is 82 km (51 miles) at its longest and 57 km (36 miles) at its widest and seems so much like Belgium at one end and Germany at the other that it is easily passed by and through in a couple of hours without much ado.

Walkers would do well to pause, for here is the densest network of footpaths, some 5 000 km (3 100 miles) of them, in the whole of Europe if not the world, offering much to savour to those who care to seek it out. Luxembourg is in many ways ideal for anyone looking for peace and quiet and walking of a gentler kind than is to be found elsewhere.

Walking in Luxembourg

Tourism plays a major role in the country's economy and, as a result, the whole footpath network is the responsibility of the Ministry of Tourism (see Useful Addresses). The Ministry takes its responsibility very seriously and the footpaths are beautifully maintained and comprehensively waymarked everywhere.

Two 'international' (i.e. European) LDFPs, the E-2 and E-3, cross Luxembourg using, as elsewhere, some of the 'national' LDFPs. Basically these national paths link the different tourist centres so that walkers can move happily from A to B knowing that food and shelter await them at the end of each day.

From the centres, there are the so-called *circuits auto-pédestres*, or *trains-pédestres*) (walks from the car or train) which average 10 km in length and make a useful 'off-day' excursion when on tour or a series of walks for a longer stay in any one centre.

Finally there are the *sentiers des Auberges de la Jeunesse* (youth-hostel paths), 15 paths which link the very fine hostels the country boasts. Most footpaths are named as in Germany. They have different symbols (circles, triangles, crosses and diamonds) and are colour-coded so that following them is rarely difficult. Differences in altitude and distances are also not too great so that, all in all, walking in Luxembourg is a very relaxing experience, without high adventure, perhaps, but also without stress.

Maps and guides

Topo-guides in the French sense do not exist, although the E-2 and E-3 are covered in the E-path guides (see page 2). The Ministry of Tourism does publish a series of small guides that cover the national paths and the *circuits auto-* and *trains-pédestres*. These take the form of booklets with maps giving starting and finishing points, the route distances, churches, spot heights and so on. Although they are by no means of Ordnance Survey standard, their scale (about 1:50 000) and their general accuracy are sufficient for you to follow routes easily.

The Luxembourg Youth Hostels Association has free maps available at a scale of 1:200 000 showing the national and youth-hostel paths. They also have descriptions in

French or German of the E-paths and maps showing walks in different regions.

Overnighting

Luxembourg has some hotels of the highest standard but also many that are modest and of more interest to walkers. It is easy to arrange demi-pension (set evening meal, bed and breakfast) so that you can make your own arrangements at midday. The Ministry of Tourism publishes a list annually showing prices and standards.

Camping is similarly organised with 'official' sites listed according to grade.

Youth hostels and *logements de vacances* (holiday homes) also appear on separate lists.

Recommended walking areas

Almost anywhere, although the eastern and northern areas which are higher offer the best walking. Clervaux with its famous abbey, Vianden, Diekirch and Ettelbruck are the best-known tourist spots in the north and centre, whilst Echternach on the river Sauer and on the edge of the Moselle wine-growing district (Luxembourg boasts some excellent white wines) will appeal to gourmets.

Climate

Generally mild with warm but not devastatingly hot summers and not too cold winters. Because of all the woodland, autumn is the very best time to go.

Hazards

None beyond the general ones (see Introduction). Dieters should beware the amounts of food and drink offered and try (but not too often) to resist the cakes. Even the Germans have been known to give them best in this respect. Non-dieters can pitch in and regret it later!

Language

Nearly all Luxembourgers speak French and German and often a third language, usually English, sometimes more. No serious difficulty therefore.

Useful addresses

>Luxembourg Consulate
>One Dag Hammarskjold Plaza
>New York, NY 10017   Tel: (212) 751-9650

>Ministère du Tourisme
>19 boulevard Royal
>1001 Luxembourg B.P. 535. Tel: 478669

or Office National du Tourisme
>77 rue d'Anvers,
>1001 Luxembourg-Ville.

for nearly all information

>Gîtes d'etape Luxembourgeois
>10 rue des Tarneurs
>Wiltz. Tel: 95022

for information on holiday lettings

>Auberges de Jeunesse Luxembourg
>18 place d'Armes
>1001 Luxembourg-Ville. Tel: 25588

for youth hostels

NORWAY

(NORGE)

A LAND where the blue-green waters of seemingly numberless fjords reflect the dramatic and rugged rocky mountains that seem to plunge vertically into their depths, where tall, fair-haired people wearing colourful folk costumes or thick, equally colourful (and now very expensive) sweaters tend neat farms perched almost defiantly on the mountain-flanks – these images of Norway are not without foundation in the holidaymaker's memory. Anybody who has walked in Norway will almost certainly be able to recall such scenes, probably with a deep sense of enjoyment and the desire to return there as soon as possible. For many hill-walkers, Norway represents the ideal in terms of scenery, of open space, of being 'away from it all' in a truly mountain environment.

This is not altogether surprising since over 70 per cent of the country is mountainous and innumerable coastal inlets weave in and out of thousands of islands, which, like the mountain areas, are uninhabited. With a population of a mere 4,000,000, concentrated in cities or where some sort of living can be forged out of the sparse agricultural terrain (3 per cent only of the total area), Norway has open space in plenty for Norwegians and visitors alike.

Walking in Norway

The Norwegians are enthusiastic outdoor people who seem

only to be waiting to get out and about at weekends or holiday times. Walking, together with cycling, fishing, sailing and bathing, is a major activity, even more so, it appears, in the form of cross-country skiing in winter.

The provision made for walkers reflects this great enthusiasm. In the first place, Norwegians have freedom of access to all uncultivated land, provided, of course, that they respect the natural environment they find themselves in. Fire-lighting in fields and forests is not allowed between mid-April and mid-September, otherwise you can go and do as you please. The only thing asked of you is that you respect private property unless a path takes you to or through it. If you are not sure, you are asked to walk or camp (a single night normally without question) at least 150 metres from it – a small price to pay, surely, for so much freedom.

The footpath network is largely geared to an extensive system of mountain huts and chalets, spaced wherever possible a day's walking apart. These paths are very well waymarked by cairns, often with a red 'T' on them, signs at bridges, junctions and so on. Map and compass work is therefore reduced to a minimum, but this does not mean you can do without it. By choosing carefully, however, you could follow such a path fairly easily, even if you lack experience. Others *en route*, especially Norwegians, will almost invariably help you if you are at all uncertain. Distances are always given in hours anyway (see Introduction), so you should be able to plan with confidence.

Walking tours, the normal 'style' of walking in Norway, exist at all levels of difficulty from following undemanding bridleways to serious mountaineering routes across glaciers and over terrain almost unexplored.

The association mainly responsible for all this splendid provision for the walker is Den Norske Turistforening (DNT), the Norwegian Mountain Touring Association (see

Useful Addresses). It will be very happy to provide you with all kinds of information, let you join one of its many tours, even organise a tour for you if you wish to go in a group.

Maps and guides

Norway is covered by maps at scales of 1:1 000 000 and 1:50 000 produced by Norges Geografiske Oppmaling (the Norwegian Ordnance Survey). All are available from DNT which also publishes sketch-maps covering all the mountain ranges in southern Norway and Finnmarksvidda in the north. The sketch-maps show the tourist lodges or huts, the cairned routes between them, hiking times (remember to add rests to these when planning) and the large-scale *Turistkarta* (special walking versions of the NGO maps already mentioned) you will need *en route*. Since these sketch-maps are free from DNT, you would do well to start with them.

If DNT does not cover the area that interests you, try local tourist offices: they often have similar publications, especially in northern Norway.

There are some guides to walks in Norway, DNT being yet again the prime source. It will always send you its pamphlet *Mountain Hiking in Norway* and you can buy from it *Mountain Touring Holidays in Norway*. This is very comprehensive and includes suggestions for walks in 18 mountain areas in southern Norway, 12 in northern Norway – enough for starters at least!

Other guidebooks to certain districts, the more popular centres and fjords in particular, exist, sometimes in English. They are best bought locally.

Overnighting

Norway has some of the most modern luxury hotels and

motels in Europe. The famous 'cold table' is a sight for sore eyes and an irresistible temptation to overeating after a day out on the fells, and comfortable rooms are the norm. Even the most modest hotels and the ferry-boats that ply the fjords are more than comfortable enough for an overnight stay.

This generally high standard of comfort is also to be found in southern Norway in the DNT's chalets and lodges. They are very fully equipped so that you only need carry a sheet sleeping bag and even this can often be hired. The DNT lodges come in three categories:

staffed lodges, supplying all meals;
self-service chalets, fully stocked with bedding, kitchen equipment and provisions for sale;
unstaffed lodges, fully equipped but with no provisions.

At the self-service and unstaffed lodges you write your own bill and leave the money in a strong-box.

In addition to the DNT lodges, there are very many private *hytter* – chalets and lodges – where you can stay for one night or which you can rent for a whole holiday. Contact local tourist offices for these.

There are also some 100 youth hostels in Norway, some specially built and very large (Oslo has 270 beds), others in farms or schools during the summer months.

The right to camp anywhere within reason has already been mentioned. It would be a courtesy even so to ask a farmer or local tenant for his agreement if he is nearby: fresh food and friendship will probably result, so it is always worthwhile.

'Official' camp sites number over 1000. They are of three standards: Very well appointed, Well appointed and Standard. A list detailing their locations and the youth hostels is available from the Norwegian Tourist Board (see Useful Addresses).

Recommended walking areas

It is usual to divide Norway into two for walking purposes: south Norway is the most mountainous, and most often visited by walkers from abroad; north Norway is more remote and 'arctic'. It requires more experience for full enjoyment. Of special interest are:

South Norway: Hardangervidda (Hardanger Plateau) south of Bergen: an undulating plateau dotted with many lakes.

Finse-Filefjell Ranges – WNW of Bergen – one of the most popular areas.

Jotunheimen – the 'Home of the Giants' with hundreds of peaks and impressive glaciers. Norway's highest peaks Galdhoppen (2 470 m, 8 100 ft) and Glittertind (2 450 m, 8 050 ft) are here; slightly to the west are the Jostedalsbreen, largest ice-cap in Europe, and the Sognefjord, Norway's longest fjord (203 km, 127 miles). Very popular for walks at all grades.

Rondane – NW of the Jotunheimen. Craggy but slightly lower (2 000 m, 6 500 ft) with many lodges at easy day-to-day distances. Good for a first visit.

North Norway: Saltfjellet (east of Bodo) – of special interest to botanist-walkers because of its flora so far north.

Narvikfjella – difficult country, more for hardened walkers and mountaineers.

Troms – great scenic variety, said to be 'Norway's Last Wilderness'.

Finnmark – a mountain plateau area inhabited by the majority of the world's reindeer Lapps.

Climate

The Gulf Stream tempers what would otherwise be a harsh

climate. Even so, winters are cold (−14°C average in the north) and summers cool but often refreshingly so. Heavy rain or snow and strong winds occur quite frequently, especially in western Norway, so go prepared. The midnight sun gives long hours of daylight in June and July.

Best walking seasons: mid June, early July and late August, early September.

Hazards

Mosquitoes, as elsewhere in Scandinavia, are a major nuisance in July and August in the marshy areas (see Introduction).

The other hazards in Norway come more from the nature of the terrain. Remember that a 2 000 m (6 500 ft) mountain often means just that because it starts literally at sea-level. The path up it, if there is one, may well start across open fields or forest but it will probably get steep and stony very quickly, stay that way for quite a time and, in the early parts of the year, finish up in snow. In other areas, crossing streams and rivers can be quite an exciting and damp adventure. Norwegian mountains are not for the faint-hearted. They demand respect and effort, so go prepared – preferably with a guide in the first instance if you are not confident of your ability to cope. If the effort required is great, the rewards Norway offers are even greater.

Language

Many words in Norwegian will have a vaguely familiar look about them, particularly for North Englanders. *Fjell* for fell, for instance, or *dal* for dale, *tjørn* for tarn. Maps are soon easily read as a result and if you do not understand the spoken language, don't worry, someone nearby is almost certain to speak English – fluently. If you speak and decide to try German with older Norwegians, explain first that you are English: some of them still have long and bitter memories.

Useful addresses

>Norwegian National Tourist Office
>75 Rockefeller Plaza
>New York, NY 10019   Tel: (212) 582-2802

- *will supply* Mountain Touring Holidays in Norway *and information on camping etc.*

>Norwegian Tourist Board
>Landslaget for Reiselivet i Norge
>H. Heyerdahlsgaten 1
>N-Oslo 1

For maps and general information

>Den Norske Turistforening (DNT)
>(Norwegian Mountain Touring Association)
>Stortingsgaten 28
>N-Oslo 1. Tel: (2) 33 42 90 or 33 11 31.

- *the fount of all wisdom for walkers in Norway. Consider becoming a member if you intend to go hut-touring and contact them first if you intend to go at all.*

PORTUGAL

On the western margin of Spain, Portugal, by far the smaller of the two Iberian countries, is, for many, lumped together with Spain as a beach-holiday country. While this is clearly true of the Algarve it belies the diversity of scenery that Portugal offers. The south is a hot, largely empty coastal plain, although there are upland areas on the Spanish border. In the north the country is mainly mountainous, with peaks to 2 000 m (6 300 ft), and deep valleys, tributaries of the River Douro. In this northern area the hills and the nearby Atlantic Ocean give a more acceptable climate for the walker than he will experience in most of the country to the south, or in Spain.

Walking in Portugal

There is no long history of hill-walking in Portugal, but a small and very enthusiastic group of activists is now making strenuous efforts to make its very attractive land better known as a walking country. This group is the walking section of the Federaçao Portuguesa de Campismo e Caravanismo (FPCC), and they are receiving help from the Serviço Nacional de Parques, Reservas e Património Paisagistico (SNPRPP), the National Service for Natural Parks. The Portuguese joined the ERA in 1982 and are anxious to link their country with the planned extension of E-3 through Spain. At present three routes (Senda de Grande

Rota) have been planned, and a one-day section of GR 1, from Beloi to Rio Mau in the Douro valley east of Oporto, and a two-day section of GR 3, from Entre to Sesimbra further south, are already marked.

In addition, shorter paths have been marked in the mountains of Serra Estrela in the centre of the country.

Maps and guides

Small guides, in Portuguese only, to the existing GR sections are available from FPCC. The guide to GR 1 is also available from Fundo de Apaio aas Organismas Juvenis (FAOJ), a youth organisation that has taken over responsibility for the path, and has a camp site at each end. The guides contain information on the path and countryside, but have only a sketch-map of the route.

A similar guide is also available from the Clube Nacional de Montanhismo (National Mountaineering Club) to the routes in Serra Estrela.

Several regional tourist offices publish local guides that include information on short walks within their areas. A specific example of this is the guide to 16 walks on the island of Madeira. Such regional guides can usually be obtained from the National Tourist Office.

The Instituto Geografico e Cadastral publishes a survey of Portugal on a scale of 1:50 000.

Overnighting

As befits a country with a developed tourist industry, there are numerous hotels of all grades in Portugal. Of most interest to the walker will be the inns and small hotels that exist throughout the country, though in some areas they are only to be found in the larger villages. The National Tourist

Board controls a number of inns, as well as a number of camp sites, and details are available from the Office. FPCC also has a number of camp sites.

There is a well-developed network of youth hostels, and the FAOJ help younger walkers with camp sites and other, cheaper accommodation.

Recommended walking areas

As Portugal is so under-developed as a walking country the walker will find new, exciting and empty areas everywhere. Of special note are the north-western corner of the country around the Natural Park of Peneda Gerês, a beautiful upland area; the Serra Estrela in the centre of the country; the Grândola mountains in the south; and the spectacular Atlantic coastline towards Cape St Vincent in the south-west corner. The possibilities offered by the Portuguese islands – Madeira and the Azores – should also be considered.

Climate

The Portuguese climate, as one might expect, is similar to Spain, but tempered by the Atlantic Ocean. As a result the upland areas are relatively mild, but very wet and cold in winter. The coastal plain can still be very hot, despite the ocean, with temperatures as high as 38°C.

Hazards

The climate must be considered a hazard, particularly in the lowland areas in summer, where sparse population centres and few drinking places, combined with high temperatures, could cause problems. Portugal also has a large population of Lataste's vipers, particularly numerous in the north-west, including the Natural Park of Peneda Gerês. While these snakes are not considered to be particularly dangerous, their bite is not trivial and care should be taken. Mosquitoes are a hazard near the coastal salt-marshes.

Language

Those who have no words of Portuguese at all will find the villagers patient and friendly, and amenable to some package-holiday Spanish. Increasingly, however, English is being taught at school and the younger Portuguese will usually be able to understand.

Useful Addresses

>Portuguese National Tourist Office
>548 Fifth Ave.
>New York, NY 10036   Tel: (212) 354-4403

for general information and a limited amount of information on camping sites, chiefly in the vicinity of the larger towns. Also some guides to specific areas.

>Serviço Nacional de Parques, Reservas e
>Património Paisagistico
>Rua da lapa 73
>1200-Lisboa

for information on Natural Parks and mountain areas

>Federaçao Portuguesa de Campismo e Caravanismo
>Rua da Voz do Operario, 1, R/C Esq.
>Lisboa. Tel: (1) 86 23 50

for information on walking and waymarked paths

>Fundo de Apaio aas Organismas Juvenis (FAOJ)
>Avenue Duque D'ávila 135/7
>1097-Lisboa

for information on GR 1

Clube Nacional de Montanhismo (CNM)
Rua Rui Faleiro
Covilhã. Tel: (59) 23364
for information on Serra Estrela and its pathways. This club can also supply information on all Portuguese mountain areas. The above address covers the central area of the country.

CNM
Rua Formosã 303
Porto
is for the northern area

CNM
Estradã da Calhaviz de Benfica
Lisboa
is for the southern area

Instituto Geográfico e Cadastral
Praça da Estrela
1200 – Lisboa. Tel: (1) 61 61 75
for maps, including a series on a scale of 1:50 000

Associacão Portuguesa das Pousādās da Juventudo
Rua Andrade Carvo 46
Lisboa 1. Tel: (1) 53 26 96
for information on youth hostels

SPAIN

(ESPAÑA)

COSTA DEL SOL, Costa Blanca, Costa Brava, Costa del Fish and Chips, flights (delayed) to Malaga, Barcelona, Palma – Spain for the tourist has become so much a matter of seaside holidays that it is easy to forget the rest of the country altogether. Easy to forget, unless the view during the flight reminds you that a great part of Spain is hilly if not truly mountainous. In fact, the dominant physical feature is the Meseta, the vast central plateau, itself some 600 m (2 000 ft) in height and surrounded by various 'sierras' or 'cordilleras' of even higher hill country. In the south, the Sierra Nevada boasts Spain's highest peak, Mulhacen (3 478 m, 11 411 ft), whilst to the north and east of Madrid a whole series of sierras rise to over 2 000 m (6 500 ft). Finally, in the far north of the country the Cordillera Cantabrica (the Cantabrian Mountains) rises quickly out of the Bay of Biscay, and the Pirineos (Pyrenees – highest peak Pico de Aneta – 3 404 m, 11 168 ft) form an effective border with neighbouring France. Were it not for the great heat that everyone associates with Spain, it might well be already one of Europe's most popular walking countries. There are signs that this facet of tourism will receive more attention in the near future. Walkers with leisure time outside the more traditional holiday periods would be well advised to watch developments closely and take advantage of opportunities as and when they arise.

Walking in Spain

Footpaths exist in the Sierra Nevada, in the coastal mountains round Barcelona, and especially in the north. The Federaciòn Española de Montañismo (Spanish Mountain Federation, see Useful Addresses) is responsible for planning and waymarking trails. It also sets up and maintains refuges in the Spanish Pyrenees. Over 1 200 km (750 miles) of the LDFPs crossing the border from France and continuing the E-3 and E-4 LDFPs have already been waymarked. Other LDFPs are being planned and developed.

Maps and Guides

El Instituto Geografico Nacional (National Geographic Institute) publishes maps at a scale of 1:50 000 covering the whole country and a few 1:25 000 maps are planned for particular areas. Walkers will find these the best maps to use.

Various guides to the more popular areas exist in Spanish and there are a few in English.

Overnighting

The splendid hotels on the Spanish coast, so much publicised in recent years for being booked up (twice over) before they were built, are unlikely to trouble walkers. Nor are the top 3–5-star hotels. Walkers are more likely to find themselves in more modest and less modern accommodation at centres inland, or in the *paradores* or *albergues* when on tour. In the higher mountains, mountain refuges might make for convenient – indeed the only – night's lodgings.

In some parts, camping will be the only possibility. Camping sites abound along the coasts and in the more popular areas inland – in the Pyrenees and round Madrid, for example. Elsewhere, they are not thick on the ground. Camping is allowed almost anywhere as a result, but there are certain conditions you need to observe. The landowner's permission to use a site is of course necessary, but it should not be within 1 km of an official site, or too near sources of drinking water or on land close to sensitive military or industrial areas. You are not always likely to know where these are, so do exercise caution before just pitching a tent for the night: you may spend the night answering questions in a military barracks if you do not.

Recommended walking areas

At present, the main areas visited by walkers are the rough, rugged peaks of the Picos de Europa, south of the Cantabrian coast, the Sierra Nevada and of course the Pyrenees, including Andorra. The Pyrenees have an atmosphere quite different from the Alps, with which they are sometimes less favourably compared. They will appeal to the naturalist-walker, especially in the central area which is a national park where bears, vultures and isards, a kind of chamois, are to be seen. As a first venture for walking in Spain, practically any part of the Pyrenees can be highly recommended.

Currently the sierras nearer to Madrid are beginning to be explored by walkers.

Climate

The shimmering scorched landscapes associated with upland Spain indicate great heat, but that depends very much on where you are and at what height. The north-west coast is wild and wet and Madrid's January average is 9°C.

In the mountains, whilst it is often sunny it is not necessarily too hot at altitude even in July and August. Thunderstorms can of course occur at any time and prolonged periods of rain can set in even in summer.

Best times for walking are May–June and early July.

Hazards

Apart from those mentioned in the Introduction, there are very few.

Language

Since Spain has worked so hard to develop tourism, language difficulties have become fewer and fewer. In the walking world, however, you will still meet many who do not understand or speak English. French is often understood and, because of the similarities, so is Italian. The tremendous invasion by Germans of recent years has tended to make German useful on occasion too.

Otherwise good acting and goodwill will ensure a ready response – certainly amongst Spanish fellow-walkers.

Useful addresses

    Spanish Tourist Office
    665 Fifth Ave.
    New York, NY 10022   Tel: (212) 759-8822

    Federación Española de Montañismo
    Alberto Aguilera 3
    Madrid 15. Tel: (1) 4451382

or   Comissió de Promoció d'Escursións
    Vallroquetes 2
    Reus

or Federació d'Entitats Excursiones
Comitè Català de Senders de Gran Recorregut
Rambles, 61
Barcelona 2. Tel: (93) 3026416/3022284
for more specific walking information

Instituto Geografico Nacional
General Ibanez do Ibero 3
Madrid 3. Tel: (1) 233 38 00
for maps in general

Editorial Alpina
Apartado de Carrear 3
Granollers
for 1:25 000 maps of the Pyrenees and Andorra and some parts of the Mediterranean coast

Club Pirinenc Andorrà
Carrer de l'Unio 2
Andorra la Vella
Principat d'Andorra
for more specific walking information

SWEDEN

(SVERIGE)

A LAND full of 'modern' if rather austere design from buildings in cities to furniture and glass, where tall, fair-haired people speaking an occasionally familiar language seem to pass the summer lying outside lakeside chalets in endless tracts of forest – these are some of the impressions of Sweden which exist in the minds of many of us. There are others. Considerable latitude in moral and social behaviour, a very high suicide rate coupled 'of course' with one of the highest standards of living in the world – to say nothing of dubious films. . . .

Like so many popular images of a country, such ideas are only partly true. They may not be all that encouraging to a walker looking for the healthy, open-air life in interesting and beautiful countryside. But, in this respect, Sweden offers a remarkable variety of landscape. Perhaps this should be expected from the third largest country in Western Europe, which extends in latitude from south of Scotland to well beyond the Arctic Circle. Moreover, a small population concentrated largely in cities means that vast tracts of the mountainous north and west of the country and even the lower-lying south and east are uninhabited. Sweden can justly lay claim to part of the last wilderness area left in Scandinavia and therefore in Europe.

Walking in Sweden

In common with their fellow Scandinavians, the Swedes are very enthusiastic proponents of the outdoor life – and for many of them, this means walking. In this, they are much assisted by the *Allemanstrat* – everyman's right – which basically gives them (and you) freedom to go wherever you please in the countryside, provided you are sensible about it. Certain obvious but minimal limitations apply and these are based on consideration for other people, animals and nature in general. You may cross private property if it is not surrounding a house or a standing crop. You may camp for one night anywhere, but if you meet the owner of your projected site, asking permission would be at least a courtesy. Gathering berries, mushrooms and deadwood is permitted outside National Parks and Nature Reserves but growing trees and bushes, rare flowers and so on are to be left alone. Fires are permitted almost anywhere if the usual precautions are taken, unless a specially built fire-place is nearby, in which case you are expected to use it. The Swedes are rightly proud of their 'open access' privilege but they respect it and accept the ensuing responsibilities. They will expect you to do the same.

It might seem that this 'freedom to roam' would discourage the setting-up of a footpath network but the Swedes' natural enthusiasm for walking plus their tourist potential has led to the creation of a number of waymarked routes. Most of these are in the central and southern 'lowland' area but a few are in the highland area in the north.

The footpaths vary in length from 20 to 500 km (12-300 miles) but are usually divided into stages of 15–30 km (9-18 miles) with some kind of accommodation at the end of each stage. Cairns, poles or marks are used to indicate the route.

The Svenska Turistföreningen or STF (Swedish Touring

Club) is largely responsible for encouraging walking activities and offers a wide variety of services to its members and to foreign visitors alike. It is the fountain of wisdom for all things to do with walking in Sweden and should be your first contact if you are going there (see Useful Addresses). The STF will also welcome you on its many guided tours if you care to join them in the holiday seasons.

Maps and guides

An information pack for most of the lowland routes is available from the National Tourist Office (see Useful Addresses) or local *turistbyraer* (offices), and the STF has similar packs for the highland routes. Most often these contain a folder, maps and information about accommodation and camping sites *en route*. Occasionally, there is a full guidebook to the route and the surrounding area.

The STF also publishes a year-book (*Fjäll-83*, *Fjäll-84*, etc.) containing up-to-date information about huts, youth hostels, footpaths, equipment, mountain-rescue and so on. It is an invaluable aid for anyone contemplating a walking holiday in Sweden.

In co-operation with the National Land Survey and a Stockholm firm, LiberKartor (see Useful Addresses), the STF has produced a series of maps for walkers, the *Nya Fjällkartan*. They cover the popular areas and are mostly at a scale of 1:100 000 with some special sheets at 1:50 000. A leaflet detailing them is available from the STF.

For the areas not covered by these maps, the Swedish National Land Survey publishes a series of 1:50 000 maps, the Topografiska Kartan 'Over Sverige'.

Overnighting

A wide variety of hotels and motels exist in Sweden. Many are run by hotel groups. Away from the towns, there are the Tourist Hotels, Country and Mountain Hotels which often provide, in addition to the usual services, organised activities, fishing, bird-watching, hiking and so on.

Of more interest to walkers is the accommodation provided by the STF. Some 9 stations, 80 chalets and mountain huts and 210 youth hostels offer accommodation along the walking routes. The simplest huts may be fairly primitive with two beds whereas the bigger huts can be quite luxurious. They are meant for *temporary* lodging (no more than two nights stay) and whilst they contain blankets, cooking equipment etc. they may not be wardened. You are on your honour to settle your account at the nearest wardened hut or station.

The hostels (open to non-members but cheaper to members of any national YHA) are of a very high standard and most often provide meals and two- and four-bedded or family rooms.

Camping is very popular and the Swedes claim one of the highest standards in Europe for their official, i.e. Swedish Tourist Board, sites. A three-star system operates and even the one-star sites offer 'hot water for dishwashing, laundering and taking a shower' so the claim may be justified. A book listing the sites, the *Campingboken*, is available at bookshops in Sweden.

Finally the sign *Rum* (room) outside a house may well save you a night out. It means just that: no meals, just a room for the night, although you may well be waylaid by the ubiquitous 'Smörgasbord' before you leave in the morning!

Recommended walking areas

South and Central Sweden have the majority of the country's waymarked routes including Skaneleden, 220 km (137 miles) 'From Coast to Coast' and the Upplandsleden, 325 km (200 miles) starting in Stockholm and going north. There is also the Siljansleden, 340 km (212 miles) around Lakes Siljan and Orsa and many more. The western part of Jämtland and Härjedalen are also recommended.

Northern Sweden – Pride of place must go to the Kungsleden – the Royal or King's Route (453 km, 293 miles), finishing (or starting) 200 km (125 miles) north of the Arctic Circle.

The National Parks (17 of them) also have routes through them, but access is sometimes restricted, especially in the breeding season.

Climate

More sheltered than Norway and tempered by the Gulf Stream, Sweden enjoys a milder climate than its latitude suggests. Summers can be quite hot but winters very cold, especially in the north-east. It can rain or snow at any time.

Best times for walking are from June to September, but late July–August might be hot and humid in some areas.

Finally, remember that Sweden is a paradise for cross-country skiing between December and April.

Hazards

Mosquitoes wherever it is hot and humid.

The terrain offers particular hazards because the walking areas are so sparsely populated. This means you must be prepared to look after yourself and know how to cope in emergencies.

Streams may have to be crossed, so you need to know the safe technique for doing this. Largely for this reason, Swedish walkers wear long rubber boots with profile soles. Lakes, too, sometimes have to be crossed: boats are usually provided, so you need to be able to row.

Language

Swedish sometimes looks like a language you nearly know but it rarely sounds like that when it is spoken. Not to worry: many Swedes understand and speak English. You may find German useful too if you have it.

Useful addresses

Swedish National Tourist Office
75 Rockefeller Plaza
New York, NY 10019   Tel: (212) 582-2802
for general information, some walking information and a Hiking in Sweden *leaflet*

Svenska Turistföreningen (STF)
Box 25
S-10120, Stockholm. Tel: (8) 22 72 00
for nearly all information about walking in Sweden, youth hostels etc.

LiberKartor
S-162 89 Stockholm Tel: (8) 739 4000

SWITZERLAND

(DIE SCHWEIZ, LA SUISSE, LA SVIZZERA, LA SVIZRA)

THE Alps and Switzerland mean quite simply the same thing for people who have never been, despite the fact that five other countries lay claim to some part of the Alps. Hazy memories of *Heidi*, St Bernard dogs rescuing marooned travellers, heroic guides rescuing marooned mountaineers from the North Face of the Eiger and colourful Swiss publicity brochures do much to reinforce these impressions. To a large extent, equating the Alps and Switzerland is not wrong: some of the most dramatic and certainly best-known Alpine peaks soar above Swiss valleys in the southern half of the country. Even in the north the Swiss plateau and the Jura mountains contain very little flat terrain, Switzerland being almost totally a mountain country where tourism is a major industry and mountain-walking is a major activity.

As a walker, you are bound, sooner or later, to find yourself in Switzerland. It is highly unlikely to disappoint you.

Walking in Switzerland

From what has already been said, it is clear that you can start walking from almost anywhere in Switzerland and find yourself in the hills. In this you will be aided by a very comprehensive network of footpaths, some 50 000 km (30 000 miles) of them, generally very well maintained and with common waymarkings nearly everywhere. With 11 independently minded and largely self-contained cantons involved in this, it might seem surprising to find such a high quality and unified system in existence, but where tourism is at stake, the Swiss are quick to unite for mutual advantage.

Responsibility therefore for footpaths and walking matters generally in Switzerland is now taken by the Schweizerische Arbeitsgemeinschaft fur Wanderwege (SAW) – the Swiss Footpaths Association. It has promoted a unified system of waymarking throughout the whole country and has also created nine national LDFPs. These traverse the country by a variety of routes which average 400 km (250 miles) in length. It is typical of the independent spirit of the Swiss that none of these routes is officially recognised as an E-path, although SAW is a very active member of the European Ramblers' Association. Perhaps the Swiss believe they can do what is best without the aid of the others – and they are probably right.

For walkers the yellow (lowland) and yellow and red or red and white (highland) marks and the neat steel signposts telling you where you are, in which direction you go next and how long it should take are soon familiar, sometimes very welcome, features of the route. You will still need a map, of course, but route-finding should not present too many problems, even if the height differences and the distances do on occasion.

You may find you have a path largely to yourself at non-holiday times and in more remote areas. At holiday times and in the popular areas, however, you will rarely walk alone. Walkers from all parts of the world are to be met with, but you will also meet the Swiss themselves for they are keen and enthusiastic walkers from childhood to old age. On such routes and at such times, 'Gruezi' or 'Gruezi mitternant' (Greetings one to another) becomes a refrain repeated a hundred times a day as you pass by.

Most footpaths are without serious danger, although they do lead to very dramatic viewpoints and somewhat airy situations on occasion. Whenever they do, safeguards in the form of fixed ropes and cables or protective rails are to be found. The Swiss, essentially sensible people themselves, will expect you to avail yourself of such aids if you need them and will offer you little sympathy and minimum help, if you do not.

Needless to say, the provision of footpath routes for all grades of walkers is a major concern of Swiss tourist centres and you will be a rare walker indeed if some route somewhere does not give you all that you could ask for – and more.

Nearly all travel and walking organisations that organise holidays abroad have centres or tours in Switzerland, so that you should be able to enjoy the experience of walking in the area of your choice without too much difficulty. The Swiss Footpaths Association itself organises many outings for its members and you would be very welcome to join them once you are there.

Maps and guides

The Eidgenössische Landestopographie or Service Topographique Fédéral – the Swiss Ordnance Survey – produces maps at scales of 1:50 000 and 1:25 000 covering the whole country. As befits a country renowned for its printing techniques, they are models of excellence showing the country in minute and accurate detail. For popular areas, e.g. Zermatt, the Bernese Oberland, special composite maps are also available.

Largely based on these official *Landeskarten der Schweiz* are many other walkers' maps. Fink-Kümmerly & Frey (see Useful Addresses) produce more than 60 special maps containing a great deal of information useful to walkers, and nearly every local tourist office in the main centres will have a map showing the walks in its area. These maps are constantly updated so it is usually better to buy them on the spot.

Guidebooks to the major LDFPs are available from the SAW including the guide to the Jurahöhenweg (the LDFP through the Juras in the north) which is the only one SAW itself does not publish.

Other guidebooks, too numerous to list in detail, exist. Most noteworthy are the *Wanderbücher* published by Fink-Kümmerly & Frey, the guides to particular areas from Bergverlag Rudolf Rother and those from Hallwag Verlag. These guides are in German and/or French.

Some guides in English also exist. The West Col guidebooks may help you in certain areas and the general guide *100 Hikes in the Alps* inevitably contains some of the so-called 'best' routes in Switzerland. A visit to your local mountain equipment shop is probably the best way of discovering what is currently available.

The Swiss National Tourist Office (see Useful Addresses) will supply a booklet, '*On foot through Switzerland*', good for starters.

Overnighting

Hotels at all grades exist, and even if they are not cheap, they usually represent good value for money. A one- to four-star categorisation of hotels is made each year by the Swiss Hotel Association and lists giving hotel details including their agreed prices are available from the Swiss National Tourist Office or local tourist offices in Switzerland. The latter will also help you with finding accommodation in hotels or private houses when you are there.

Mountain huts mostly run by the Swiss Alpine Club are usually set high and are really intended as refuges for mountaineers intent on high-level climbing. They vary from simple shelters to large elaborate establishments and when wardened will usually provide drinks. They are not really suitable for walkers on tour but often make a worthwhile day's walk from a centre. Membership of an alpine club is recommended if you intend to sleep in them on several occasions.

At lower levels, some 100 houses run by the Friends of Nature are available for those who become members and youth hostels provide for those under 25 years of age.

Camping is extremely popular and there are some 450 official sites as well as numerous private ones. With the owner's permission, you will be able to camp in certain other places, but always make sure that camping is not forbidden: penalties for breaking the law in this respect can be severe. As ever, camp site lists are available in tourist offices.

Recommended walking areas

'Everywhere' and 'anywhere' would be almost the only, possibly the best, answers to give for Switzerland. Obviously the Alps take pride of place and certain areas are more popular than others. Once you know them, you will know why, but if crowds are not for you, do try to visit them off-season if you can. Amongst the best are:

The Bernese Oberland – Famous centres like Interlaken, Grindelwald and Kandersteg and mountains like the Jungfrau, Eiger and Mönch abound. Also good for walking tours.

The Valais – Zermatt with perhaps the best-known mountain shape in the world, the Matterhorn above it, is only one of many other well-known centres like Arolla and Saas-Fee.

The Grisons (Graubünden) – South-eastern Switzerland

has some quieter valleys but also very famous resorts like Arosa, Davos, Klosters and St Moritz.

The Ticino (Tessin) is the less rugged area, joining on to the Italian Lakes with Locarno and Lugano as major centres. Good for gentler (and warmer) walking.

Climate

Alpine and Central European – which means cold winters with a great deal of snow and warm summers with some periods of rain and always a risk of thunderstorms. It can be gloriously hot for quite long periods in July, August and September and these are probably the best times to go if good weather is important to you. Remember, however, that big mountains make their own weather and it can change from one range or valley to the next.

Hazards

None except those mentioned in the Introduction.

Off the paths, mountain terrain can become hazardous and the cost of mountain-rescue is very high in Switzerland. Make certain you are well insured before you go.

Language

The majority of the Swiss understand German and some speak a version of it. This 'Schwyzer Deutsch' is known to confuse the Germans so you may have difficulty from time to time. Fortunately, the Swiss also learn Hochdeutsch (High, i.e. 'normal', German), French and Italian. In the Lake Geneva area French is the usual language and in the Locarno–Lugano area Italian is spoken. Romansch – derived from Latin – is spoken by a very small group in south-eastern

Switzerland. In all tourist areas, English is widely understood and spoken.

Useful addresses

Swiss National Tourist Office
608 Fifth Ave.
New York, NY 10020   Tel: (212) 257-5944
for much information, guides, maps (including Schweizerwanden, *a map showing the LDFPs)*

Schweizerische Arbeitsgemeinschaft für Wanderwege (SAW) (Swiss Footpaths Association)
In Hirshalm 49
CH-4125 Riehen. Tel: (1) 49 15 35
for guides to LDFPs and up-to-date information on them

Schweizer Alpin Club (SAC)/Club Alpin Suisse (CAS)
Helvetiaplatz 4
CH-3005 Bern Tel: (31) 43 36 11

Schweizer Touristenvereien, 'Die Naturfreunde' (TVN), Amis de la Nature (AN)
Birmensdorferstrasse 67,
CH-8036 Zurich Tel: (1) 23 99 83
for huts

Schweizerische Camping and Caravanning-Verband (SCCV)
Fédération Suisse de Camping et Caravanning (FSCC)
Habsburgerstrasse 35
CH-6000 Lucerne Tel: (41) 23 48 22

Schweizerischer Bund für Jugendherbergen (SJH)/
Fédération Suisse des Auberges de la Jeunesse
Postfach 132
Hochhaus 9
CH-8958 Spreitenbach Tel: (56) 71 40 46

Eidgenössische Landestopographie/Service Topographique Fédéral
Seftigenstrasse 264
CH-3084 Wabern Tel: (31) 54 13 31

Fink-Kümmerly and Frey
Gebelsbergstrasse 41
D-7000 Stuttgart 1
Tel: (0711) 64 30 91

for maps

WEST GERMANY

(BUNDESREPUBLIK DEUTSCHLAND)

WEST Germany conjures up, for many, pictures of rolling hills and valleys covered in dark pine forests, and sprinkled with villages full of medieval buildings. This is, to some extent, true of the centre, but there are miles of sand dunes on the coast, and open heath in the north. To the south there are dramatic Alpine peaks offering a wide variety of landscapes. Almost everywhere walkers will find all kinds of interests and attractions.

Walking in West Germany

For many Germans *das Wandern* – walking, rambling, a longing to wander out into the wide world of nature – is almost a way of life. It is certainly a, and perhaps the, major national pastime. There are few German households where a rucksack, old or very new, and at least one pair of walking boots are not to be found. School rambles are a normal, often mandatory, part of the curriculum.

It should be no surprise therefore to find that some 155 000 km (97 000 miles) of footpaths exist, most of them very well maintained and very fully waymarked. And it would be unusual to walk very far on most of them and not meet a German fellow walker or, more likely, walkers, since the Germans are very gregarious walkers, and the club outing, especially on Sundays, is a strong and much respected tradition. As a stranger you are likely to be given a very warm welcome, an invitation to join them if you are going the same way, and a staggering amount of information about the surrounding country. Do not hesitate to accept such an invitation. The experience can enhance any holiday and may well bring you friends for life.

Almost inevitably, there are a bewildering number of walking clubs in the BRD. The national umbrella organisation, the Verband Deutscher Gebirgs und Wandervereine (see Useful Addresses), boasts 48 member-organisations and there are many more that do not belong to it. The VDGW will supply the names and addresses of its member organisations, but little else.

For local information you will have to write to the clubs responsible for footpaths, lodgings, club-huts (*Wanderheime*) and information for their area.

This manifestation of the *Land* mentality, which creates intense local pride and activity but sometimes evokes little response to requests from outsiders, is both the curse and the blessing of German life. Your request for information may be ignored, or it may bring an avalanche of paper. Once on the spot, however, you will almost invariably be given a hearty welcome.

Whatever else, the walking possibilities are endless: LDFPs (*Fernwanderwege*), circuit paths (*Rundwanderwege*), nature trails (*Naturpfade*), short afternoon strolls, even 'keep fit' paths (*Trimmdichpfade*) where physical exercises are posted at intervals of a few hundred metres, just in case the walking is not enough.

There is no nationally agreed system of waymarking except for the E-paths, three of which cross the BRD. Footpaths are, however, generally so well maintained, and colour-coded so fully, that with the appropriate map and guide there should be no difficulty in following a route. Forest paths sometimes cause problems, but not often.

In addition to the E-paths, there is a system of major paths (*Hauptwanderwege*) up to 200 km (125 miles) long and often named after some famous local personage or, very likely, walker. From these, minor paths branch off to link with another *Hauptwanderwege* or to villages, places of interest, or the ubiquitous 'viewpoint' (*Aussichtspunkt*), very much like a major and minor road system.

Signposts tend to give times to destinations, but sometimes distances in kilometres are given, sometimes both.

Maps and guides

As might be expected, these exist in all shapes and sizes. Official maps at scales of 1:25 000 or 1:50 000 are the responsibility of each *Land* through its *Landesvermessungsamt*, of which there are 11.

In addition to these, which must be ordered or bought in the Footpath Edition (*Ausgabe mit Wanderwegen*), there are many private publishers. The ones most used by walkers are: *Alpenvereinskarte*, published by the German and Austrian Club (DÖAV) and recommended for Alpine areas, and *Kompass-Wanderkarte*, published by Heinz Fleischmann GmbH – probably the most familiar to anyone who has walked in the German-speaking countries.

There are many others. In Germany it is merely a question of choosing from the vast array. When ordering from abroad those suggested would be 'safe', and will provide sufficient planning information.

Guidebooks are also very numerous. Two of the best known are: Deutscher Wanderverlag (Dr Mair and Schnabel and Co.), a fairly new firm with an impressive list of titles already, and Fink-Kümmerly and Frey, the major publisher of guidebooks in German. Bergverlag Rudolf Rother also publish guides, mainly for the Alpine areas.

Overnighting

Everywhere there are good hotels of every grade and, for walkers, the small *Gasthaus* or *Gasthof* is often a 'best buy'. The signs *Privatzimmer* or *Zimmer zu vermieten* (rooms to let in private houses) are often worth investigation, and can lead to inexpensive and memorable experiences.

Youth hostels in Germany are mainly for the under-25s. They can be used by the older tourist from abroad, but they do have certain restrictions that can be irksome.

The other major outdoor activity of the Germans, camping, is catered for in over 1900 official *Campingplätze*, which vary from the ultimate in luxury to the very simplest possible. Camping is allowed on private land, if the owner's permission is obtained, but in the nature parks and some forest areas to camp outside the official sites is *verboten*.

Recommended walking areas

Most of the walking in West Germany is not difficult, and every area has its attractions. The Central Upland area gives the most typically German *Wandern*, and each range (*Gebirge*) will easily provide enough walking for almost any length of holiday. Specially recommended are:

In the North: Lüneberger Heide, Harzgebirge, Fichtelgebirge and Böhmerwald – the Bohemian Forest.

In the Centre: Sauerland, Eifel, Taunus and Odenwald.

In the South: Schwarzwald (Black Forest), Schwäbische Alb (Suabian Alps) Bayrische Alpen (Bavarian Alps).

Climate

The North and Baltic Seas affect the coastal areas so that winters are cold and summers mild. In the central region the climate is continental, fairly severe in winter and hot in summer, sometimes oppressively so, and with consequent thunderstorms.

The German Alps have the usual Alpine weather, with long snowy winters and short, hot summers with rain and thunderstorms on occasion.

Hazards

The major hazard is rabies (*Tollwut*). Warning notices are to be found where it is particularly rife. *Never* tangle with wild or stray animals, and remember that even scratches can be fatal.

Language

English is easily understood in most centres of information and is widely spoken by younger people. Many older Germans often speak German only, and a dialect at that, and most publications are in German, although most map legends include an English key.

Useful addresses

>German National Tourist Office
>630 Fifth Ave.
>New York, NY 10020   Tel: (212) 757-8570

for regional information, write to the Landesverkehrsbüro in the region you wish to visit, or, for specific towns etc., to the Fremdenverkehrsbüro. This is often situated in the town hall (Rathaus).

>Deutscher Alpenverein (DAV)
>Praterinsel 5
>D-8000 München 5. Tel: (089) 29 3086

or Verband Deutscher Gebirgs und Wandervereine
Falkerstrasse 70
D-7000 Stuttgart. Tel: (0711) 295336
for specific walking information and a list of member organisations

Deutscher Camping Club
Mandlstrasse 28
Postfach 40 0428
D-8000 München 40. Tel: (089) 33 4021

Deutscher Jugendherbergswerk (DJH)
Bülowstrasse 26
Postfach 220
D-4930 Detmold. Tel: (05231) 31091

for youth hostels

Maps and guides:

Geo-Center – Internationales Landkartenhaus
Honigwiesenstrasse 25
Postfach 80 08 30
D-7000 Stuttgart 80. Tel: (0711) 75 50 31

or Liebherrstrasse 5
D-8000 München 22. Tel: (089) 22 62 45

for all maps and guides. Geo-Center publishes a map Katalog *of over 800 pages. It might cost more than the maps you order, so beware!*

Deutscher Wanderverlag
Dr Mair and Schnabel and Co.
Haussmannstrasse 66
D-7000 Stuttgart 1. Tel: (0711) 43 78 13

Fink-Kümmerly and Frey
Gebelsbergstrasse 41
D-7000 Stuttgart 1. Tel: (0711) 64 30 91

Bergverlag Rudolf Rother
Landshuter Allee 49
Postfach 667
D-8000 München 19. Tel: (089) 16 00 81

YUGOSLAVIA

(JUGOSLAVIJA)

ALTHOUGH most tourist publicity creates an image of sun-drenched beaches along its considerable Adriatic coastline, Yugoslavia has for the walker far greater attractions inland. Enough has been written, or dramatised, about the heroic partisan struggles in this part of Europe for nearly everyone to know that, inland, Yugoslavia is a country of vast forests topped by soaring mountains of bare limestone, gleaming white in the sun.

In fact, some 75 per cent of the country is mountainous. The great bow of the Alps terminates in the north in the Kamnik, Karavanka and Julian Alps, where Triglav, Yugoslavia's highest mountain (2 864 m, 9 394 ft) dominates its neighbours. Further south the forests of the Dinaric ranges gradually give way to limestone plateaux and in the south-east the Rodopi mountains extend from Bulgaria into Macedonia and Serbia.

Much then for the walker to explore in Yugoslavia, and every year sees yet another area of its hill country on offer for walking holidays.

Walking in Yugoslavia

The Yugoslavs themselves are very enthusiastic walkers and, well aware of the tourist potential, have developed and maintain about 6 000 km (3 750 miles) of waymarked footpaths on which lie some 160 mountain huts. These are mainly the responsibility of the Planinska Zveza Slovenije (the Slovenian Alpine Federation) or the Institute of Forestry (see Useful Addresses).

Some of the routes are very long and strenuous: the Slovene Mountain Traverse, for instance, crosses the highest peaks of the Julian Alps and continues to the Adriatic. Some sections involve rock-climbing or scrambling and certainly require a good head for heights and are for the experienced only.

The European footpath E-6 has been extended into Yugoslavia where it is known as the E-6 YU. It enters the country from Austria at Radlje and ends some 250 km (155 miles) later at Kastav on the Adriatic near Rijeka. Anyone obtaining the red and yellow booklet at the beginning describing the route and following the red-circle with yellow dot waymarks to the end via the 36 checkpoints is given a badge and diploma to prove he has done it.

Please note: several of these paths lie within a National Park where walking is allowed during daylight hours only, and where, for reasons of conservation, you are not allowed to deviate from the path.

Maps and guides

Maps at scales of 1:20 000 and 1:50 000 are available from Planinska Zveza Slovenije for the areas where waymarked routes exist.

Guides to the E-6 YU and the Slovene Mountain Traverse in English are also available from the same source. The Alpine Federation also publishes a guide to nearly forty routes, varying from a half-day to several days walking, in the Julian and Karavanka Alps.

Other guides in Slovene, not the easiest language to understand, exist and are published by the alpine associations of other regions.

Overnighting

Yugoslavia possesses some exceptionally luxurious hotels, specially built for, and much frequented by foreign tourists. Hotels are divided into five classes: L (De luxe), A, B, C and D and pensions into first, second and third class.

Rooms in private houses, classified by price, and apartments and villas for rent are also available.

Camping is allowed on official sites only unless a special permit is obtained from the local tourist office, in which case certain areas outside the sites may be used.

Information about overnighting is available from local tourist offices (which will often help you to find accommodation) or from the National Tourist Office (see Useful Addresses).

Recommended walking areas

At present, most walking activity is in the northern (Alpine) areas, as far as foreign walkers are concerned. The development of winter sports holidays in the central highlands may well reveal further areas of interest for walking at other times of the year.

There are signs that the travel organisations that offer walking holidays are busy exploring further possibilities. Lake Ohrid in the extreme south is already popular and others on the coast south of Split with walking in the hinterland are also appearing.

Climate

Like the different regions, the climate is very varied. The Adriatic coastline boasts over 2000 hours of sunshine per year, whereas in the mountains the weather is Alpine. Snow can be expected here from December until the end of March (the 1984 Winter Olympics take place in Sarajevo).

Best times to go walking are spring and autumn.

Hazards

In addition to those mentioned in the Introduction, one or two need to be mentioned.

Insects (especially mosquitoes) can be a nuisance in humid places in high summer. The Yugoslavs estimate that as well as thousands of herbivores (deer, chamois etc.), there are about 300 bears and 80 lynx in their protected nature reserves. Unless you stalk them deliberately you are not likely to come within photographing distance, and, unless you tread on one having a snooze, within biting or mauling distance!

On the high limestone peaks, water can be very, very scarce. You may need to carry more drink than usual to stay comfortable.

Language

Six socialist republics and two socialist autonomous republics make up Yugoslavia. There are also people who claim Albanian, Hungarian, Turkish, Slovakian and Ruthenian descent. Not only you but also the Yugoslavs can therefore have language difficulties.

Serbo-Croat is the most widely spoken language followed by Slovene and Macedonian. English is spoken in the more popular tourist areas and German (it is sometimes wise to say you are British) is often spoken or understood. Otherwise good acting might be *de rigueur*.

Useful addresses

Yugoslav National Tourist Office
630 Fifth Ave.
New York, NY 10020   Tel: (212) 757-2801

All the main towns and tourist centres have information offices:
Planinska Zveza Slovenije
Dvorzakova 9,
61001 Ljubljana. Tel: 312 553
for maps, guides and other walking information

E-6 YU Committee
Gozdorski Institut (Institute of Forestry)
Vecna Pot 30
61000 Ljubljana
for information on the European LDFP E-6 YU and other information

EASTERN EUROPE

(ALBANIA, BULGARIA, CZECHOSLOVAKIA, EAST GERMANY, HUNGARY, POLAND, ROMANIA, USSR)

IT would have been much more satisfactory to have dealt with each Eastern European country separately. Sadly, the various difficulties that arise when one tries to visit them, especially as an individual walker, preclude such treatment. Not that the potential and possibilities for walking are nonexistent. Far from it: each of the countries listed above has walking of very particular interest and walkers galore. It is just that, if you go, you are almost certain to find yourself on a highly organised tour and without the sense of freedom that some walkers find essential to their enjoyment.

If, however, you are prepared for or enjoy walking in a group, then these countries might offer you experiences every bit as enjoyable as those elsewhere.

The system seems to be that the group arrives at a well-known holiday resort where 'your guide for the holiday' meets you and takes over. Much depends on this person. If he or she is the standard tourist guide, interested in visiting famous monuments, churches, 'dollar' shops and so on, your walking holiday will not be the best walking trip you ever had. The tourist authorities are, however, always alert to the needs of their foreign visitors and always anxious to improve their services. As a result, you may find you have a guide especially interested in and enthusiastic about walking, even specially trained for such work. In this case, you will very probably have a memorable holiday despite the sometimes irksome 'conditions' that accompany it in varying degrees. You may find, for instance, that just when you have planned an off-day, breakfast is at six o'clock because the party has to catch the cable-car at 7.50 some ten miles away and it is the only one on which you are allowed to travel. A particular ridge may attract you because the weather looks perfect for it, but since the programme says that the day is for bird-watching or visiting the local partisan monument, this is what you must do. Individual whims are sometimes catered for, but rarely without difficulty. The best advice is to go along with your hosts: you and they will enjoy the holiday much more – and you may get your way more easily in the long run.

Walking in the East European countries

In most East European countries, mechanised transport is hardly abundant, so walking is a stark necessity in everyday working life. It might seem strange therefore to find people walking for pleasure, but this is the case, and you will find very many people out and about walking in all the popular areas at holiday times. What will almost certainly be lacking is the plethora of sophisticated equipment that seems to have become essential in Western Europe. If you are a safety-conscious walker – and we hope you are – the footwear you see will at times appal you. This is probably not the case in Czechoslovakia (some of their boots imported to Britain are well worth looking at if you want good value for money), but you will find people in smooth, leather-soled town shoes on exposed, airy places in the Polish Tatras, for instance, and in the marshy, steep valleys descending from the Bucegi Plateau in Romania. If you really want to make friends for life in Eastern Europe, take any spare walking equipment along as a present: it will be highly prized and accepted with wild delight.

The East European countries that are trying to develop their considerable tourist potential have realised the importance of good footpath networks. As a result, you will find good routes well waymarked nearly everywhere. The usual system relies on colour coding with colours on the map corresponding to waymarks on the paths. Sometimes the paths are numbered too. As you might expect in countries where the state is largely in control, the paths are the responsibility of a government department, the forestry authority, national park authority or the local tourist board. You would not be wrong to think that most of these authorities will expect you to stay on the paths and not wander about at will. There is rarely anything sinister in this. It is usually done from the best of motives: environmental protection. More than elsewhere, the 'Forbidden' notice needs to be heeded very fully: an on-the-spot fine may be one of the consequences you pay for not doing so. The routes will, however, take you to more than enough spots to satisfy you, so there is no point in upsetting your hosts. Needless to say, your own protection is almost invariably safeguarded by way of fixed ropes etc. when the going gets tough.

Maps and guides

Maps vary from fairly simple ones showing the footpaths and major features like summits and mountain huts to quite elaborate maps more or less up to OS standards. Usually, a special tourist map will be on sale when you arrive and the various tourist offices in Britain (see Useful Addresses) should be able to tell you if they cannot supply it themselves.

The Czechs publish a *Guide to the High Tatras* in English which is excellent but we have not been able to trace any other guides in English. Guides in human form, as already mentioned, exist everywhere. Very often they are trained mountain guides with a wealth of expertise and often a West European language (English and German are very common) as well. Do accept their services if offered: there is no better way of learning about the country and making good friends.

Overnighting

Specially built 'tourist hotels' are now a common feature of East European countries. They offer very high standards of comfort, in the main. If on a centre holiday you do not find yourself in such a hotel, then you are likely to find yourself in a perhaps even more imposing but older building that almost certainly did not begin life as a hotel. Many summer residences from palaces to chalets were taken over after the Second World War and are now used to accommodate tourists. They may not be up to the highest modern standards, but are much closer to the authentic way of life of the country. The food probably will be as well. On balance, their appeal to walkers, aiming to find out about a country in a way other kinds of tourist cannot, should be greater.

Apartments and chalets are sometimes available for rent, but as yet this is largely confined to the more popular resorts. Rooms in private houses rarely, if ever, seem to be on offer.

Mountain huts and refuges vary a great deal in size and quality. They rarely match the standards set by Austrian or Italian huts, but those are exceptional anyway. If you intend or get the chance to use them, do find out before you set off what the prevailing situation is regarding booking, meals, equipment etc. The national or local tourist authorities will tell you.

Camping, not unexpectedly, is allowed on official sites only. Again the national or local tourist offices will supply you with information.

Recommended walking areas

Albania – At present, Albania remains a country little interested in our kind of tourism. Walkers who wander into it by mistake – and survive to wander out again – would be very welcome contributors to a future edition of this guide!

Bulgaria – Now developing fast as a skiing country, Bulgaria should soon be offering very interesting possibilities to walkers. It has mountain ranges 'west of centre', the Stara Planina (Balkan Mountains) and the Sredna Gora and in the south-west the majestic Rodopi Mountains rising to 2 925 m (9 600 ft) at Bulgaria's highest peak, Mount Musala. These last will be the ones to visit for good walking.

Czechoslovakia – Provision for walkers is very good, which is hardly surprising since Czechoslovakia consists largely of the Central European Highlands.

In the west of the country are the Sudetens, Moravian Heights, the Ore and Giant Mountains and, bordering on West Germany, the Bohemian Forest.

In the east, the High Tatras, bordering on Poland, are the mountains most visited by tourists from Western Europe. Fine rugged mountains rising to above 2 000 m (or 6 500 ft; the highest summit is Gerlachovasky at 2 655 m, 8 710 ft), they have a fine and very well developed network of huts, chalets and colour-coded footpaths.

East Germany – is starting its 'hiker-tourist' drive in the near future and will not reveal plans before then. Routes, 1:50 000 maps and a 200 km (125 mile) LDFP are known to exist, and since the western and southern borders are continuations of much that is good in West Germany, the 'drive' could produce interesting possibilities – if it is not too forced.

Hungary – Much of Hungary is low-lying plain, but in the north lie the Carpathian foothills. The Hungarians are anxious to develop the tourist potential of their country and walkers would be welcomed with open arms. The Hungarians admit, however, that they still have much to do in making suitable provision. Perhaps it is the place to visit before it tries too hard!

Poland – Walkers are most likely to be pointed towards the Tatras (highest peak Rysy – 2 499 m, 8 198 ft) bordering on Czechoslovakia. A favourite walking area and a National Park, it has a well-developed network of huts and colour-coded footpaths. The mountains offer walking at all grades including some very airy and exciting routes. If you are in a group of more than ten, the National Park will make you an offer you can't refuse of a (free) mountain-guide – accept gracefully and enjoy the experience.

Romania – Walkers will probably find themselves in the Carpathians, around (but not in, we hope) Dracula's Castle of Bran in the Transylvanian Alps or in the Bucegi. The Bucegi is plateau country, not very interesting on the top but with some fine gorges descending into the main valleys and the tourist hotels.

Walker-naturalists will want to visit the Danube delta, especially at bird migration times, but remember that Black Sea fever killed more troops in the Crimean War than the battles. With much untreated sewage now being dumped into the Black Sea, the risks may actually have been increased.

USSR – Some West European mountaineers have managed to visit the Caucasus in the past twenty years and found the walking activity highly regimented. Of course, the Caucasus mountains are serious stuff and perhaps the Russians have very good reasons for imposing stringent safety regulations on those who wish to explore them.

A huge network of footpaths does exist and is used by Soviet walkers and climbers, but these are 'not available' at present to visitors from other countries.

Climate

Most of the area has a Central European climate, more extreme than that further west. Summers are generally hot with violent thunderstorms, winters very cold with long periods at or below freezing – hence the development of skiing.

Best seasons would be early summer and late autumn.

Hazards

Apart from those mentioned in the Introduction, the hazards most likely to spring to mind from media reports are human in form. Unless you deliberately set out to provoke or behave in a stupid manner, you will find these hazards largely imaginary but you should carry identity documents with you at all times just to be sure. More than one country in Western Europe expects you to do the same.

Language

Apart from the obvious difficulties of unfamiliar Slavic languages, there are the problems of different meanings for the same word. 'Democracy' is the classic example and 'access' might be another. German is often a help. French too on occasion and in Romania (the language has a Latin base) Italian is a great help.

For the rest, good sign language and goodwill usually evoke a warm and very friendly response.

Useful addresses

> Bulgarian Tourist Office
> 50 E. 42nd St.
> New York, NY 10017
> Tel: (212) 661-5733

English Department
Balkantourist
1 Lenin Square
Sofia

Czechoslovakia

Czechoslovakian Travel Bureau
10 E. 40th St.
New York, NY 10016   Tel: (212) 689-9720

East Germany

East German Embassy
1717 Massachusetts Ave. NW
Washington, D.C. 20036   Tel: (202) 232-3134

Hungary

Ibusz Hungarian Travel Bureau
630 Fifth Ave. Room 520
New York, NY 10020   Tel: (212) 582-7412

I.B.U.S.Z.
1364 Feiszabadulas
Ter 5
Budapest

Poland

Polish National Tourist Office
500 Fifth Ave.
New York, NY 10036   Tel: (212) 354-1487

Romania

Romanian National Tourist Office
573 Third Ave.
New York, NY 10016   Tel: (212) 697-6971

Ministry of Tourism
Department of Publicity
7 Magheru Boulevard
Bucharest

USSR
    Intourist Information Office
    630 Fifth Ave.
    New York, NY 10011 Tel: (212) 757-3884

LANGUAGE AND TRAVEL BOOKS FROM PASSPORT BOOKS

"Just Listen 'n Learn" Language Programs
Complete language programs to learn Spanish, French, German and Italian.

"Just Enough" Phrase Books
Travelers' phrase books available in Spanish, French, German, Italian, Greek, Dutch, Portuguese, Serbo-Croat, and a special 8-language, multilingual edition.

"Getting Started" Books
Introductory language books for Spanish, French, German, and Italian.

"Welcome" Books
Welcome to Spain
Welcome to France
Welcome to Ancient Rome

Grammar References
Spanish Verbs and Essentials of Grammar
French Verbs and Essentials of Grammar
German Verbs and Essentials of Grammar
Essentials of Russian Grammar

Dictionaries
Vox Spanish and English Dictionaries
Harrap French and English Dictionaries
Klett German and English Dictionaries
Everyday American English Dictionary

Technical Dictionaries
Complete Multilingual Dictionary of Computer Terminology
Complete Multilingual Dictionary of Aviation
 and Aeronautical Terminology
Complete Multilingual Dictionary of Advertising, Marketing,
 and Communications

Verb References
Complete Handbook of Spanish Verbs
Spanish Verb Drills
French Verb Drills
German Verb Drills

Humor in Five Languages
The Insult Dictionary: How to Give 'Em Hell in 5 Nasty Languages
The Lover's Dictionary: How to Be Amorous in 5 Delectable Languages

Other References for Language and Travel
Guide to Spanish Idioms
Guide to Correspondence in Spanish
Español para los Hispanos
Business Russian
Everyday Conversations in Russian
Hiking and Walking Guide to Europe

PASSPORT BOOKS

Trade Imprint of National Textbook Company
4255 West Touhy Avenue
Lincolnwood, Illinois 60646-1975 U.S.A.